John Jay

THE FORGOTTEN FOUNDER

John M. Pafford

HERITAGE BOOKS
2009

HERITAGE BOOKS
AN IMPRINT OF HERITAGE BOOKS, INC.

Books, CDs, and more—Worldwide

For our listing of thousands of titles see our website
at
www.HeritageBooks.com

Published 2009 by
HERITAGE BOOKS, INC.
Publishing Division
100 Railroad Ave. #104
Westminster, Maryland 21157

Copyright © 2009 John M. Pafford

Other books by the author:

How Firm a Foundation: William Bradford and Plymouth

Two Christian Commonwealths: William Bradford's Plymouth and John Winthrop's Massachusetts

Cover: Portrait of *John Jay (1745–1829), c.1858*
Courtesy of John Jay Homestead State Historic Site
New York State Office of Parks, Recreation and Historic Preservation

All rights reserved. No part of this book may be reproduced or transmitted in any form or by any means, electronic or mechanical, including photocopying, recording or by any information storage and retrieval system without written permission from the author, except for the inclusion of brief quotations in a review.

International Standard Book Numbers
Paperbound: 978-0-7884-5009-9
Clothbound: 978-0-7884-8189-5

Acknowledgments

To my wife, Martha, I express appreciation for her unstinting loving support for my writing this biography and for carefully proofing it. Our daughter, Dana Peringer Moutz deciphered my handwriting (no small task), expertly keyed the manuscript into the computer and sent it on its way to Heritage Books.

Table of Contents

Foreword vii
Preface xi
Chronology of John Jay's Life xiii
Part I: The Life of John Jay 1
    Beginnings 3
    The Road to Independence 11
    War for Independence 29
    In New York 47
    President of the Congress 59
    Spain 67
    The Treaty of Paris 73
    Secretary for Foreign Affairs 85
    The Constitution 95
    The Federalist Papers 121
    Chief Justice 127
    Jay's Treaty 135
    Governor of New York 145
    The Bedford Years 155
    End Notes 163
Part II: The Character of John Jay 173
    The Bible 175
    Faith 179
    Christian Practice 183
    The Church 187

Christianity and Government 191
Principle and Party 197
Son and Sibling 203
His Education 207
Marriage 211
As a Father 217
Personality 223
Friendship 229
Courage 235
Professional Life 241
Power and Authority 245
Loyalty and Revolution 251
War and Peace 255
Slavery 261
Indians 267
Retirement 273
Death 277
End Notes 283
Part III: The Legacy of John Jay 289
The Lessons of Leadership 297
Endnotes 299
Bibliography 301

Foreword

For people of faith and all others of good will looking for historical role models of statesmen at the time of the American founding, John Jay (1745-1829) is sure to inspire and instruct. Of all the major founders of that important era, Jay was arguably the most religiously devout and intentionally integrated Christian among them. His faith was the guiding star of his political ideals and public actions as well as his personal and family life. Not only did Christianity direct his ethical behavior with moral precepts, but Jay's faith informed his understanding of the world as created by God and infused with meaning, as directed toward an ultimate end and purpose by Divine Providence, as fallen due to mankind's moral rebellion, and as redeemed by the Savior who recreates a new humanity for the eventual restoration of the world and its consummation in God. In other words, John Jay comprehended the implications of a Christian worldview for all of life—personal, professional, and public.

    A native of New York, Jay was raised in the Christian faith by loving parents and reared in the English piety of the *King James Version* of the

Bible and Anglican *Book of Common Prayer*. His family tree is comprised of the major currents of the Reformed Tradition, and this heritage, no doubt, informed his spiritual and intellectual development. The family's religious history was Huguenot, and their storied identity was forged by the experience of persecution in France. England, and later its colony of New York, provided Jay's ancestors with refuge and safe haven for religious, civic, and economic freedom. The Jay family thrived and enjoyed the material prosperity of their adopted home.

    Classically trained by Anglican clergymen at the King's College in New York—later Columbia University, Jay was afforded one of the best educations available in the New World. He attended King's with the sons of privileged and prominent New York families, and after his graduation in 1764 he studied and practiced law. The "high tide in the affairs of men" on the eve of the American Revolution swept Jay into government service. He began his political career at the age of 29 as a Member of the first Continental Congress in 1774. In that famed Congress which met in the new Carpenter's Hall at Philadelphia, Jay was a front-bencher at the head of the conservative phalanx that checked the radical spirit of some of its members from Virginia and Massachusetts. From that spotlight forward Jay's principled conservatism informed his political thought and actions as a legislator, jurist, diplomat, and chief executive. Retiring from public office in 1801, Jay was the only principal founder to serve his country continuously for 27 years. His patriotism and fidelity to America and its political ideas are manifest.

Jay's life and public service bear witness to a man motivated and animated by an ethic of neighbor-love. Evidence of his selfless dedication and duty to his country is demonstrated by his service as a Member of Congress, Chief Justice of New York, President of the 2nd Continental Congress, Minister to Spain, Paris Peace Commissioner, Secretary of Foreign Affairs for the Confederation Congress, first Chief Justice of the United States, Special Diplomatic Envoy to Great Britain, and Governor of New York. Jay's public service, however, did not end with government service. Throughout his career and to the end of his life he was active in many religious, moral, and charitable causes including the abolition of slavery, the reorganization of the Anglican Church in the United States in the aftermath of the American Revolution, and the distribution of Bibles throughout the world by the American Bible Society.

Dr. John M. Pafford's new biography *John Jay: The Forgotten Founder* is a very welcome correction to the dearth of recent scholarship on Jay. It rightly restores Jay to the pantheon of American founders whose lives and leadership all of us can ill-afford to forget. For to do so, would be to forfeit the religious, economic, and political liberties that the Revolutionary generation bequeathed to us and to our posterity. Pafford's biography presents a compelling and integrated study of the American founding and its political first principles through a well-focused lens on the life and leadership of Jay. The pages which follow are sure to inspire its reader with the absorbing story of a great American statesman.

Alan R. Crippen II
President
The John Jay Institute for Faith, Society and Law
April 29, 2009

Alan R. Crippen II is the founder and president of the John Jay Institute for Faith, Society and Law, a para-academic center committed to developing future leaders of character like John Jay for principled public leadership. Mr. Crippen is a graduate of Westminster Theological Seminary and an Anglican Clergyman.

Preface

Of the most significant Founding Fathers—George Washington, Alexander Hamilton, John Adams, Thomas Jefferson, James Madison, Benjamin Franklin, and John Jay—Jay is the least known today. Yet at one time, he was considered by many to be the logical successor to Washington as chief executive of the new country. His résumé is the most impressive of those who did not serve as president. Among the positions he held were: president of the Continental Congress, minister plenipotentiary to Spain, member of the peace commission which negotiated the 1783 Treaty of Paris, secretary for foreign affairs, co-author of *The Federalist*, first chief justice of the United States Supreme Court, and two term governor of New York. In retirement, he was president of the American Bible Society.

As the third century of American history develops, it is essential to renew our knowledge of and respect for the beliefs upon which this country was founded and the great men who propounded them. It is hoped that this study of John Jay will play some small part in this endeavor.

Chronology of John Jay's Life

1745 December 12—John Jay born in New York City.

1760 Matriculated at King's College in New York City.

1764 May 22—Jay graduated with a bachelor of arts degree, gave a speech at graduation.

1767 May 19—Jay was awarded a master of arts degree by King's College.

1768 October 31—He was admitted to the bar in New York and began the practice of law.

1774 April 28—Jay and Sarah Van Brugh Livingston were married.

1774 July 28—Jay was elected one of New York's delegates to the First Continental Congress.

1775 April 20—He was elected to the Second Continental Congress.

1775 November 3—He was commissioned a colonel in the New York militia.

1776-1777 Jay headed counter-subversion efforts in New York and organized spy activities.

1777 May 3—Jay was elected chief justice by the New York Provincial Congress.

1778 November—Governor George Clinton asked Jay to return to Congress to represent New York; the legislature approved.

1778 December 10—Jay was elected president of the Continental Congress.

1779 September 27—He was chosen by Congress to serve as minister plenipotentiary to Spain.

1780 January 22—He went to Spain.

1781 June 15—Congress elected him one of the American peace commissioners in Paris.

1782 November 30—Preliminary articles of peace signed.

1783 September 3—The final terms of the Treaty of Paris signed.

1784 May 16—Jay left Paris, returned to the United States through England.

1785 Jay was a leader in forming the New York Manumission Society and was elected its first president.

1787-1788—Jay, Alexander Hamilton, and James Madison wrote *The Federalist.*

1789 September 26—He became the first chief justice of the United States Supreme Court.

1794 He negotiated the Jay Treaty with the British.

1795 Jay resigned as chief justice and was elected governor of New York, serving two terms.

1801 He retired to his estate in Bedford.

1802 Sally died.

1822 Jay accepted election as president of the American Bible Society.

1829 May 18—Jay died.

PART I: The Life of John Jay

All flesh is as grass, and all the glory of man as the flower of the grass. The grass withers, and its flower falls away, but the word of the Lord endures forever.[1]

Nothing is more certain than the indispensable necessity of government; and it is equally undeniable that whenever and however it is instituted, the people must cede to it some of their natural rights, in order to vest it with requisite powers.[2]

The Life of John Jay

Beginnings

The first of the Jays to settle in the New World was Augustus (1665-1751), grandfather of John, who came seeking religious freedom after King Louis XIV revoked the Edict of Nantes in 1685, making Roman Catholicism the only legal faith in France. The Jays, a prosperous Huguenot (Protestant) family, now suffered the consequences of their belief with the seizure of the family's property in La Rochelle.

At first Augustus went to England, then crossed the Atlantic to settle in New York. There he was successful in business and won the hand of Anna Maria Bayard (1670-1756) whose father was Gov. Peter Stuyvesant's nephew and also was descended from Huguenots, his family having fled France to the Netherlands back in the sixteenth century. Her mother was the daughter of Govert Lookermans, reputed to be the richest man in New York. Van Cortlands, Van Rensselaers, and Schuylers were among her cousins.

The couple had four children who reached adulthood, Peter (1704-1782) being the only son. Peter Jay became a prosperous merchant under the training of his father, engaged in the importation of cloth and textiles from England and the Netherlands plus flax seed from Ireland and exporting timber, wheat, and furs. He also traveled to England and to France.[3] He married his mother's second cousin, Mary Anna Van Cortland (1705-1777). Of this union were born ten children, seven of whom lived to be adults: Eve (1728-1810), Augustus (1730-1801), James (1732-1815), Peter (1734-1813), Anna Maricka (1737-1791), John (1745-1829), and Frederick (1747-1799). Four of them suffered serious mental or physical problems: Eve had emotional problems as a girl, Augustus was mentally retarded, and Peter and Anna Maricka both lost their eyesight to smallpox in 1739. Shortly after John's birth, the family moved from Manhattan to Rye on Long Island Sound. Rye then was a small town near the Boston Post Road (later U.S. 1). The family farm was about four hundred acres, extending down to the water. From all indications, it was a great place for a boy to grow up. A love of the rural life would remain with Jay. With both their parents representing wealth and influence and Peter personally amassing a fortune, the children grew up in comfortable, privileged circumstances. As was common with people at this level of society, the Jays were members of the Church of England (today the Episcopal Church). Young John would develop a deep Christian faith. He, his father, and his grandfather all served as members of the vestry at Trinity Church in New York City. This venerable parish was incorporated in 1697. George Washington attended services there during the time he spent in the city.[4]

His parents believed strongly in the value of a sound classical education. During his preschool years, his mother taught him English and Latin. Peter Jay was a good father, strict but affectionate and proud of young John's accomplishments, as demonstrated in his letters. Of Mary Jay little is known, no letters by her having been found. She appears to have been a good wife, mother, and homemaker in spite of less than robust health. John was tutored privately until the age of eight when he entered a grammar* school in New Rochelle headed by the Rev. Peter Stroupe. Born in Switzerland, he had pastored a Huguenot church in Charleston, South Carolina before converting to the Church of England and moving to New Rochelle, a community of largely Huguenot background, less than ten miles from Rye. Here Jay's fluency in French developed.

After three years studying there, he returned home to complete his college preparatory education

---

* Normally boys attended grammar schools from ages eight to fourteen; then they either entered universities or apprenticeships.

under the tutorship of George Murray. On August 29, 1760, the fourteen-year-old John entered Kings' College, now Columbia University. As part of the entrance requirements, he had to demonstrate ability in Latin and Greek grammar, read the first three books of Virgil's *Aeneid*, the first three of Tully's *Select Orations* both in Latin, and translate the first ten chapters of the Gospel of John from Greek into Latin.[5]

King's had been founded largely through the efforts of Church of England members. In 1746, the New York legislature authorized a lottery to raise funds for the college and in 1753 voted five hundred pounds from excise duties for the following seven years. A majority of the board of trustees members would belong to the Church of England. Furthermore, Trinity Church donated a tract of land with the stipulation that the president of the college must be a communicant of the Church and that the Book of Common Prayer would be used in chapel services. This Church control continued until well after the end of the Revolutionary War. In July 1754, classes began under the leadership of Dr. Samuel Johnson, widely regarded at that time as the most learned of the colonial clergy. In October of the same year, a royal charter was granted the college.[6]

In 1762, Jay's older brother James, an alumnus of King's, was sent to England on a fundraising campaign for the college. He had studied medicine in Edinburgh, at that time the foremost medical school in the Western World, and had been admitted to the College of Physicians and Surgeons. He now secured royal consent to have collections taken in Church of England parishes if approved by the local clergy. George III personally gave four hundred pounds. James succeeded well, collecting almost six thousand pounds, and was knighted for his achievement.

Shortly before his graduation in 1764 occurred an event which demonstrated Jay's sense of honor, determination, and rather legalistic turn of mind. He was present when some students, due either to high spirits or resentment of the steward at the college, began to break up a table in the dining room. Myles Cooper, who had taken over as president in 1762, headed the investigation. When the students were interrogated, no one identified the culprits or admitted to knowledge of the incident. Jay, though, stated that, although he knew who did it, he would not answer the questions. The students were called before a faculty committee and reminded of their having agreed to obey college regulations. Jay again declined, maintaining that his refusal to answer did not constitute a violation of the code. The faculty disagreed; the students, Jay included, were suspended, but permitted to return in time for graduation. On May 22, he was awarded his B.A.,[7] being one of two students chosen to give salutatory addresses.

Rather than being drawn into the mercantile world of his father and grandfather, Jay determined to enter the legal profession. His legalistic turn of mind was discussed previously in reference to the King's College incident. More significant, though, was his recognition of the need for a civilized society to be based on Christian precepts and supported by a sound judicial system rooted in the Bible. As an attorney and in public service, he would do his part to further order, justice, and freedom.

He now began clerking and reading law in the office of Benjamin Kissam, one of the most prominent New York attorneys. During the day, he drafted wills and deeds and assisted in preparing cases for court. In the evening, he read in Kissam's library. On October 26, 1768, Jay was admitted to the bar and began a three year partnership with his friend Robert Livingston, Jr. It was dissolved amicably with the consent of both parties and Jay began a successful solo practice. His reputation was enhanced by his ably serving during 1769 as clerk of the royal commission charged with solving the boundary dispute between New York and New Jersey.

At the same time Jay's professional career was moving in the right direction, his personal life too was flourishing. He was tall and slender with sharp features. Although studious and on occasion rather aloof, he had a fun-loving side and a good sense of humor, sometimes verging on the ribald. He fell in love with Sarah Van Brugh Livingston, the very attractive, vivacious daughter of William Livingston, later governor of New Jersey, and distant cousin of his former law partner. The sentiment was reciprocal and they were married April 28, 1774, beginning a long, happy union which produced two sons and five daughters. Eleven years younger than he, Sally, as she was known, was the perfect wife for a rising public figure; an excellent hostess, charming, a fashion style-setter, her spirited personality countered her often pompous husband.

In addition to his own growing family, Jay bore responsibility for his retarded brother Augustus and the blind siblings Peter and Anna Maricka. The neurotic Eve married a Loyalist clergyman who deserted her when the Revolution began. Jay then undertook the responsibility to raise their son, Peter Jay Munro, as his own. All these things he did not do just from a sense of responsibility, but willingly from Christian love, becoming increasingly involved as his parents grew older. His other two brothers were not much help. Frederick attempted to follow his father's path in business, but, his talent and his success were more limited. James, or Sir James, was a substantially different problem. More capable and successful than Frederick, he did not rise to the level of John and appeared jealous of him, sometimes to the point of hostility. He did help the American cause by developing an invisible ink and a chemical solvent which made the writing readable. This procedure was used to good effect by American spies and diplomats. There were times, though, when questions arose as to which side James really supported. For example, after serving in the New York legislature, he became disenchanted with the rebellion and arranged for his capture by the British. Later taken to England, he tried unsuccessfully to establish himself as an American representative for peacemaking purposes, coming up with a plan for a new union which would grant more autonomy to the Americans; it was rejected by the British. Finally, though, he ended up back with the Americans, and, in fact, treated John Adams in Paris for influenza after the peace treaty had been signed.[8]

The Road to Independence

Meanwhile, relations between the British government and the American colonies worsened after the British victory over France in the Seven Years War, known in North America as the French and Indian War. Now that the French had lost Canada, the colonists no longer felt threatened and, consequently, felt less dependent on British armed forces. A number of predictions were made that this loss of fear would lead to a growing move toward independence. For example, in 1763, Charles Gravier, Comte de Vergennes, later foreign minister of France, stated that:

> Delivered from a neighbor whom they always feared, your other colonies will soon discover, that they stand no longer in need of your protection. You will call on them to contribute towards supporting the burthen which they have helped to bring on you, they will answer you by shaking off all dependence.[9]

There is much truth in this, although other factors were significant in leading to the colonial decision to declare independence.

At the 1754 Albany Congress, a gathering of delegates from seven colonies—Massachusetts, New Hampshire, Rhode Island, Connecticut, New York, Pennsylvania, and Maryland—and the Iroquois Confederacy, met at the behest of the British government to discuss the anticipated war with France. At the Congress, Benjamin Franklin proposed a plan of colonial union under the crown. Representative bodies in each colony would elect members of a Grand Council presided over by a president general appointed by the monarch. This new government would have no jurisdiction over the internal affairs of any colony, being limited to external matters such as war against the Indians, taxes to pay for it, buying land from them, and setting up new colonies in the West. The proposal, however, was rejected by both the British government and the colonial assemblies. Both opposed the establishment of a new government, the former fearing too much colonial freedom would result and the latter concerned that they would lose too much freedom.[10] The colonies had not yet suffered enough aggravation at British hands to see the need for national unity.

John Jay: The Forgotten Founder

The British success in the Seven Years War led to their becoming the most powerful colonial empire in the world, but also doubled their national debt. Because of Indian problems on the western frontier, 10,000 British troops would be stationed in North America.* Not unreasonably, the British government, headed by George Grenville, believed that the colonies should bear more of the financial burden. The problem, though, was how they determined to do it. Parliament passed the Stamp Act; on March 25, 1765 it was given royal assent. This legislation required the colonists to purchase tax stamps for legal documents and publications, even playing cards. This was objectionable to the colonists since for the first time an internal tax (as differentiated from trade duties) was imposed on the colonists without the involvement of a colonial legislature. The British Parliament was acting as an imperial Parliament without any representation from the empire, violating the traditional British principle of "no taxation without representation."

Massive opposition to the Stamp Act now developed on this side of the Atlantic, culminating in a boycott of British goods. Also, prominent Bri-

---

* As colonial restiveness grew during the decade before independence, these forces increasingly would be concentrated in major population centers, especially Boston, in order to maintain order and British authority.

tish figures, such as William Pitt, Edmund Burke, Adam Smith, and William Wilberforce, opposed the arbitrary action of the Grenville ministry. Burke, a member of Parliament and one of the greatest political thinkers in the history of Western Civilization, served as Rockingham's secretary. He was convinced that the British government was violating British constitutional principles and common sense by taxing the colonies directly without giving them parliamentary representation, forcing them to choose between supporting the sovereignty of Britain and freedom:

> If that sovereignty and their freedom cannot be reconciled, which will they take? They will cast your sovereignty in your face. Nobody will be argued into slavery.[11]

Added to this was pressure from British merchants hurt badly by the boycott. As a result, the Grenville ministry fell in August and was replaced by one headed by the Marquis of Rockingham. In March 1766, the Stamp Act was repealed. Overlooked in the rejoicing was the fact that at the same time Parliament passed the Declaratory Act, asserting their right to pass whatever laws they wished concerning the colonies.

In August, Rockingham resigned and Pitt again became prime minister. Now, however, his great days were behind him; hit by manic-depression and gout, the Duke of Grafton replaced him, Charles Townshend, chancellor of the exchequer, being the real power in the administration. In June 1767, the Townshend Act was passed levying duties on English imports entering the colonies such as tea, glass, paper, and paint. To placate colonial ire, Parliament removed duties on colonial grain and whale oil shipped to Britain. Enforcement of trade regulations now was to be more efficient. Townshend died in September and was replaced by Lord North.

From 1768-1770, the colonies again erupted against British regulation.* Non-importation agreements spread and there was even some rioting. The boycott was quite effective in Boston, New

---

*At this time, the population of the colonies was about 2,600,000. Virginia was the largest with 504,000 people followed by Massachusetts at 337,000, Connecticut 298,000, Pennsylvania 270,000, Maryland 255,000, North Carolina 247,000, New York 193,000, South Carolina 170,000, New Jersey 122,000, New Hampshire 81,000, Rhode Island 58,000, and Delaware 37,000. (Dorothy Denneen Volo and James M. Volo, *Daily Life During the American Revolution* [Westport, Connecticut: Greenwood Press, 2003], 8.)

Philadelphia, populated by 40,000 people, was the largest city in British North America. Next was Boston at 17,000, then Charleston with 12,000 and Newport 11,000. (*Ibid.*, 9.)

York, Pennsylvania and New Jersey, but not so in Virginia, Maryland and the Carolinas. A growing number of colonists was moving into the independence camp at the same time many others were moving in the opposite direction, their fear of mob rule leading them to conclude that British rule clearly was preferable.

The Duke of Grafton resigned as prime minister in January 1770, Lord North taking his place. The Townshend duties now were repealed except for that on tea. The radicals in the colonies, though, were not placated and in England those who wanted to make sure the colonists knew who was in charge were gaining strength. In between were those such as Jay who stood for order and justice, but regarded the British government as too arbitrary and wanted more autonomy within the empire. Eventually this would prove to be an untenable position; those who held it would be pulled either into the independence movement or into total support of Britain.

During the seven years of Jay's private practice, his views on the growing movement for independence had not fully crystallized. He was a conservative who believed, as Russell Kirk later set forth, that a civilized society must have order, justice, and freedom. The sequence is essential; without order, nothing can function. Once order is established, justice can come into being and once order and justice prevail, freedom can flourish. Jay was concerned with the danger that mob rule could result from the actions of some of the advocates of independence. Apropos of this was his statement in a letter to George Washington on June 27, 1786 that:

> The mass of men are neither wise nor good, and the virtue like the other resources of a country, can only be drawn to a point and exerted by strong circumstances ably managed, or a strong government ably administered.[12]

Here is expressed not just conservative beliefs, but the Biblical teaching about the sin nature—that people are born with inclinations to sin and that they must change through coming to Christ as Savior and Lord. No one has to teach children to be self-centered, to take whatever attracts them, and to lie to gain advantages or to avoid trouble. Virtue and civilized behavior are acquired; they are not innate. Jay, along with others such as Washington, Alexander Hamilton, and John Adams, believed that a strong government was a better means of fostering order, justice, and freedom than a weak one.

His father and brothers, however, were early supporters of the anti-British position as was his father-in-law. His practice included both Tories, also called Loyalists (supporters of continuing as part of the British Empire) and Whigs (advocates of independence). As a good attorney, he represented both faithfully and skillfully.

The same concern for order and justice led John Adams to defend the British soldiers put on trial for murder following the so-called Boston Massacre of 1770. On March 5, a mob in Boston harassed a British sentry. Eight soldiers led by Captain Thomas Preston reinforced him. The mob now turned violent, throwing stones, chunks of ice, snowballs, and oyster shells. Shots were fired into the crowd, although it is not clear that Captain Preston gave the order, and five men were killed. Separate trials were held for Preston and the enlisted men. There being no proof that Preston gave an order to fire, he was found not guilty. In the second trial, six soldiers were also found not guilty while two were convicted of manslaughter, being branded on their thumbs the extent of their sentence.

Adams did blame the quartering of soldiers in Boston for being an irritant, but clearly condemned the mob not the soldiers for the incident. People such as he and Jay opposed the high-handed policies now being implemented by the British government, but worried about the possible breakdown of order and justice which could ensue were a revolution to break out. Jay, however, was slower than Adams in concluding that independence was necessary.

In December 1773, a mob in Boston, incensed by the tea duty and aroused by speakers such as Samuel Adams, dumped 324 chests of tea into Boston harbor. The British government responded the next year with the Coercive Acts: the Boston Port Act which virtually closed that port until damages were paid; the Massachusetts Government and Administration of Justice Acts which essentially ended self-government there; and the Quartering Act which authorized the forced quartering of soldiers in private homes.

At the same time, the Quebec Act gave the conquered French Roman Catholic inhabitants of that province freedom to retain their religion, language, and local customs within the British system. Furthermore, the border of Quebec was extended south along the Connecticut River to 45° latitude, thence west across Lake Champlain to the St. Lawrence River where it turned southwest through Lake Ontario and Lake Erie, then further west to the Mississippi River, finally finishing by moving north to Hudson Bay. This vast western region now was sealed off from further development by the American colonies. This antagonized many Protestant colonists to their south who had fought them long and hard; the Americans feared this could be the beginning of further restrictions on them. In the fevered atmosphere of the time, almost any conspiracy theory could gain adherents. Opposition to Britain grew throughout the colonies, leading to united action.

Loyalists, those who rejected a break with Britain, were motivated by a variety of factors. For many, loyalty to the crown was a deeply held principle. There also was the apprehension that revolution would lead to a breakdown of civilized order. There further was the fear that war would disrupt the lucrative trade that flowed in and out of cities such as New York, Philadelphia, and Charleston. For some people, as on the Virginia frontier, opposition to the independence-minded tidewater aristocracy led lower class individuals to advocate loyalism. Support for independence and for staying British cut across socio/economic class lines, preventing the struggle from becoming a class war.

Jay was elected to the First Continental Congress which convened in Philadelphia on September 5, 1774. At twenty-eight, he was one of the youngest delegates. The delegates were selected by revolutionary committees or conventions in all the colonies except Georgia, the one in which Loyalist sentiment was strongest. New York and South Carolina also were powerful centers for that position. The call for independence was most influential in Virginia, Maryland, Delaware, and Massachusetts, although the Loyalists had a significant voice in the latter colony. Loyalists opposed the Congress and were not among the delegates. The fifty-five men who comprised the First Continental Congress ranged from those wanting independence now, such as Samuel Adams of Massachusetts, to those critical of the arbitrary actions of the British government but believing that the problems could be solved short of breaking the unity of the empire. Jay was in the latter camp.

One of their key leaders, Joseph Galloway of Pennsylvania, proposed a plan of union. Established would be an American Parliament, equal to the British Parliament, each having veto power over the other on matters pertaining to this side of the Atlantic. As it was being debated, word arrived of the Suffolk Resolves adopted by a convention of the towns in the area of Boston. They declared the Coercive Acts null and void, called for Massachusetts to declare its independence from the

United Kingdom, urged the people to take up arms, and wanted economic sanctions imposed on the British. Congress backed the Suffolk Resolves and defeated the Galloway Plan by a single vote. Jay and other conservatives were on the losing side.

Jay continued to be cautiously optimistic about a successful resolution of colonial grievances without resorting to war. Negotiation with the British was the approach he preferred. If this did not work, trade sanctions then would be tried. If both failed, war would be the final recourse. As part of his determination to further freedom peacefully, he authored for Congress the "Address to the People of Great Britain," an attempt to influence British opinion against the government of Lord North. It was adopted October 21, 1774. In it, Jay contended that the colonists were entitled to all the rights of Englishmen and that the British Parliament had no right to act as if there were no limits to its power over the colonies. There was, however, no change in British policy as a result of this effort.

The outbreak of fighting at Lexington and Concord in April 1775 did not bring Jay into the independence camp; he still hoped for a peaceful solution—autonomy for the colonies within the British Empire—as the Second Continental Congress convened in May 1775. A majority of the delegates also advocated a settlement short of independence. If London would yield its intransigent position that Parliament could levy direct taxes on the colonists and exercise direct control over them and if more autonomy were granted, then the colonial firebrands could be restrained and imperial unity maintained. At this stage, Jay moved that another petition be sent to George III; it was seconded by John Dickinson of Pennsylvania. In it independence was rejected as the end being sought. Jay had been willing to suggest that the British could negotiate with the colonial assemblies rather than with Congress. This Dickinson removed, realizing that Congress never would vote for a proposal which bypassed it. This "Olive Branch Petition" was adopted after acrimonious debate. Backers of independence supported it, convinced that London would reject it and because they wanted no break with Dickinson and others who opposed British policies, but still had hope. This was Jay's last hope to avoid war.

Indicative of his growing disenchantment with the British, on November 3 Jay was commissioned colonel of the 2nd Regiment, New York Militia of Foot. Although he would have some military involvement and be engaged in anti-subversion and counter-intelligence activities during the campaigning around New York in the early part of the war, most of the wartime years found him in Congress or on diplomatic assignments in Spain and France.

On November 9, word arrived in Philadelphia that George III would not receive, let alone consider, the "Olive Branch Petition." This convinced Jay that nothing could be gained from further talk. He was part of a delegation, including George Wythe of Virginia and Dickinson, sent by Congress to talk New Jersey out of its plan to try a petition of its own. He argued convincingly that all Americans must stand united and that Congress should act for all. Now he was convinced that independence was the only option left for those who wanted freedom.

Could war between Britain and the American colonies have been averted? From the vantage point of the colonies, only an acceptance of American subordination would have placated George III and those chosen by him to lead the government. Only a dramatic change in British policy could have changed history. Perhaps if William Pitt the Elder had retained his mental and physical health and lived longer, a rapprochement could have been effected. He opposed harsh treatment of the colonies such as taxing them without giving them representation in Parliament. Significant other prominent figures such as Edmund Burke and Adam Smith also opposed British colonial policy. In a speech delivered on May 22, 1775, just a few weeks before Lexington and Concord, Burke stated that:

> First, Sir, permit me to observe, that the use of force alone is but temporary. It may subdue for a moment; but it does not remove the necessity of subduing again: and a nation is not governed which is perpetually to be conquered.[13]

He further commented in the same address about Americans that "A love of freedom is the predominating feature which marks and distinguishes the whole" and that "This fierce spirit of liberty is stronger in the English colonies, probably, than in any other people of the earth."[14]

But, Pitt's health failed and George III and his minions who were determined to put the colonists in their place controlled the government; war now became inevitable.

In June 1776, the Continental Congress began serious moves to separate from the United Kingdom. A committee was appointed to draft a declaration declaring independence. It consisted of Thomas Jefferson of Virginia, John Adams of Massachusetts, Benjamin Franklin of Pennsylvania, Roger Sherman of Connecticut, and Robert

Livingston of New York. Jefferson was assigned the task of writing the declaration; the committee members altered it, but in general Jefferson's wording formed the final draft. On July 4, with final passage, independence was official and a new country came into being. Over five years of bitter combat with frequent lost battles and many frustrations lay ahead, though, before that independence would be secured.

Among the most powerful forces in the battle of ideas was Thomas Paine's *Common Sense* which in 1776 set forth powerfully and clearly the reasons independence was necessary and right. Paine, an Englishman, had come to the colonies in 1774, quickly establishing himself as an effective voice for creating a new country. At first, he was hailed widely, including by George Washington and John Adams. *Common Sense* sold between 150,000 and 200,000 copies in a land whose population then was about 3,000,000—most impressive circulation. Later, Paine's slashing rejection of Christianity and his political radicalism* led to chasms appearing between him and many who previously supported him. Among others he attacked was Jay, referred

---

* For example, he spurned the conservative philosophy of Edmund Burke, supported the French Revolution (until he was imprisoned and came close to being guillotined), and attacked Washington's military and political leadership.

to by Paine as "always the sycophant of everything in power,"[15] a ridiculous slur. Someone such as Jay, who was both a Christian and a Federalist, was anathema to Paine, but in 1776 these conflicts still were below the horizon. Paine would prove to be one of those individuals good at stirring up revolts, less good at constructive building.

The Life of John Jay

War for Independence

Before proceeding with Jay's political, diplomatic, and counterintelligence activities during the conflict with Britain, it would be well to pause briefly and consider how the war developed militarily.

The theater of operations through which the war would rage was vast—about 1200 miles from north to south along the Atlantic seaboard and extending inland about 250 miles. Since rail travel had not yet developed and hard surface roads were few, water was the best way to move military units relatively quickly and easily, making control of ports, rivers, and lakes significant. For most of the war the British navy dominated, a key period in the autumn of 1781 being a sharp exception.

After Lexington and Concord in April 1775, the British were blockaded in Boston by the colonial forces, mostly from the aroused towns of Massachusetts. The New England colonies had implemented the English militia system from the beginning of their settlements, the danger of Indian attack necessitating a warrior attitude. All able-bodied males between sixteen and sixty received at least rudimentary training and mustered periodically for more. George Washington of Virginia, a veteran of fighting against the French and the Indians, was chosen by the Continental Congress in June to command the new army, partially out of respect for his ability, partially to demonstrate that the conflict was national, not just involving New England. His was a commanding presence. He was tall, 6'2" or 6'4"—historians differ—muscular with broad shoulders and great stamina. There was an aura of command about him, palpable to all who encountered him. He cultivated a persona, for example wearing his Virginia militia colonel's uniform to meetings of the Congress and exuding the bearing of the aristocrat. But, he was what he presented himself to be. His integrity, dedication to principle, and courage in combat were outstanding. Although not an intellectual as were Hamilton, Adams, and Jefferson, he was a man of intelligence and common sense. As a general, he grew, learning from his mistakes, tempering his aggressive nature as he came to realize the necessity to keep an army in being, not to risk it unnecessarily. He was a good strategist and improved as a tactician. For example, his 1776 strike at Trenton was a bold stroke of genius and his 1781 campaign from New York to Yorktown brilliant in conception and execution.

John Jay: The Forgotten Founder

To secure control of Boston and the harbor, the British commander, General Thomas Gage, ordered the newly arrived General Sir William Howe to seize two heights, Breed's Hill and Bunker Hill on the Charlestown peninsula just north of the city. This he did on June 17 (prior to the arrival of Washington), but at heavy cost only after two assaults had been repulsed and the outnumbered Americans had run out of ammunition. Over forty percent of the British were killed or wounded. A period of relative calm now ensued as both sides built up their strength, neither one being able to win a decisive battle.

During this period, a remarkably audacious operation was mounted by Benedict Arnold, a great general who combined strategic vision with heroic battlefield leadership, but whose later defection to the British made him one of the most reviled men in American history. On September 5, he moved his men from coastal Maine up the Kennebec River to strike at Quebec from the south. There they were to link up with General Richard Montgomery who would use the familiar Lake Champlain route and seize Montreal on his way to the rendezvous. The British did not believe it possible for a sizable military force to reach Quebec over the virtually trackless route chosen by Arnold. The surprise was lost, though, when the Indian carrying a message from Arnold to General Philip Schuyler took it instead to General Sir Guy Carleton who commanded the British army in Canada. The astonished Carleton was able to get reinforcements to Quebec and stave off a desperate attack by the Americans under the cover of a snowstorm on December 31. During the attack, Montgomery was killed and Arnold badly wounded, dooming any chance for victory by the now decimated Americans.

Had the assault succeeded, it is breathtaking to conjecture how history might have been altered. After all, during this time, whoever controlled Quebec controlled the St. Lawrence River and whoever controlled the St. Lawrence controlled Canada. There could have emerged a single gigantic country stretching from the Arctic Ocean to the Gulf of Mexico. But, it was not to be. The following spring, the Americans retreated south by the Lake Champlain route and Canada was safely British. Again, Arnold demonstrated skillful and courageous leadership, fighting a naval action on Lake Champlain that checked any further British advance during that year.

Meanwhile, back in Boston, Gage had been replaced by Howe. Then, on March 2, 1776, Washington seized Dorchester Heights south of Boston, making the British position untenable. On March 17, they withdrew to Halifax, Nova Scotia. From there, Howe moved his forces south and defeated Washington in several battles on Long Island and Manhattan during the summer and fall, forcing the Americans into New Jersey then further south and west into Pennsylvania. Washington kept his army in being through these defeats, being aided in withdrawing from Long Island to Manhattan by a providential rainstorm and morning fog which shielded the operation from British eyes and by the cautious tactics of Howe. Capable general the latter may have been, but he had suffered heavy losses in the direct attack at Bunker Hill and he had no desire to quash brutally those for whose complaints he had a degree of sympathy. An opponent of the British government's American policies, he was, nonetheless, a loyal subject of the crown and a good professional soldier.

Washington suddenly turned on his pursuers on Christmas day, a time when armies traditionally were in winter quarters; he moved a small force across the Delaware River by night during a snowstorm which masked their approach and smashed a brigade of Hessians in British service at Trenton early the next morning. Then on January 3, he routed a British contingent at Princeton. These two small tactical gems restored sagging American morale and let their enemies know that the war was far from over. Of this campaign, Frederick the

Great of Prussia, no mean general himself, stated that:

> The achievements of Washington and his little band of compatriots between the 25th of December and the 4th of January, a space of ten days, were the most brilliant of any recorded in the annals of military achievements.[16]

The following year, the British set in motion a well-conceived plan to divide New England from the rest of the country, subdue it, and then defeat the remainder. On February 16, 1777, General John Burgoyne, a veteran officer with a gallant record, submitted to the British government a proposal to accomplish this end. He called for a force to move south from Canada along the line of the Sorrel River, Lake Champlain, and Lake George to the Hudson River where it would join at Albany a force under General Sir William Howe which would move up the Hudson from New York. A third force under Lt. Colonel St. Leger was to strike out from Oswego on Lake Ontario, advancing east along the Mohawk River to Albany.

The plan was essentially sound. The Canadian force could travel by water for all except a few miles of their route. Once the juncture of the three forces had been effected, the New England states could have been cut off from the rest of the country and reduced without being able to receive effective reinforcement from the other parts of the country. If the central and southern states did not choose to submit, they could be subdued much more easily with the north eliminated.

Unfortunately for the British, the order issued by Lord Germaine, secretary of state for war, to Howe, commanding in New York, instructing him concerning his role in the plan, was misplaced. Howe, who was lukewarm concerning the idea, preferring to focus primarily on the capture of Philadelphia, did not consider himself bound by the plan. In a day of slow communication, the difficulties in coordinating far flung operations across an ocean were many. Adding to the British problems was the fact that Lord Germaine was not a capable military leader nor was he well-respected.

On June 21, Burgoyne moved south at the head of about 8,200 well-trained, experienced officers and men. The first major objective, Ft. Ticonderoga on Lake Champlain, fell easily to the British since the Americans under Colonel St. Clair had failed to fortify a key hill, Mt. Defiance or Sugar Hill, which dominated their positions. When the British occupied the hill, St. Clair regarded his position as untenable and retreated to the south-east. Burgoyne followed up the retreating Americans, striking sharp blows at them, but moving into more difficult country to the east of Lake George. Rather than returning to Ticonderoga in order to follow the Lake George route to the Hudson, Burgoyne decided to strike directly through this region. This decision cost him ten or twelve days during which the Americans were able to bring up reinforcements and to prepare a warm reception for the invading British.

Meanwhile, Washington had surmised correctly the British plan and had sent General Benedict Arnold and Colonel Daniel Morgan with his contingent of riflemen to reinforce General Philip Schuyler, a capable officer who commanded the American forces opposing Burgoyne.

As the British moved south, their lines of communication grew longer and more vulnerable. Furthermore, they lacked the vehicles necessary to carry with them all the supplies needed for a protracted campaign. It was necessary, therefore, to send out an expedition to round up cattle and horses. Lieutenant Colonel Baum, a German officer in British service, commanded the approximately 700 men who struck east to the Connecticut River country. On August 16, Baum was attacked by 1,500 New Hampshire militiamen commanded by Colonel John Stark, an experienced and able soldier. After a hard-fought battle, the British were driven from the field. After the conclusion of the battle, 550 British reinforcements arrived under the command of Colonel Breyman, too late to aid Baum, but in plenty of time to be defeated themselves. Burgoyne fully realized the import of this defeat. The Americans were proving to be formidable adversaries and his supply problem was increasingly serious. He resolved to push on, depending on Howe and St. Leger to link up with him at Albany.

The force under St. Leger advanced down the Mohawk Valley as planned with 850 soldiers and 1,000 Indians. New York militia units under General Nicholas Herkimer which attempted to block them were defeated.

When Schuyler learned of St. Leger's approach, he sent Arnold with 1,200 men to intercept the invaders. Arnold, knowing that the Indians treated lunatics with great respect, arranged for a demented Mohawk Dutchman to take word to St. Leger's camp that a superior number of Americans was advancing on them. At this the Indians fled, leaving St. Leger with no good alternative but to retire, ending the threat from this prong of the British offensive.

Meanwhile, Howe had moved by sea to the Chesapeake Bay with his main force in order to seize Philadelphia. General Sir Henry Clinton, left in command at New York, had been informed by Howe: "If you can make any diversion in favour of General Burgoyne approaching Albany . . . I need not point out the utility of such a measure."[17] These words did not constitute an order and reflected Howe's lukewarm attitude. Furthermore, Clinton's forces were inadequate to provide for the security of New York and to mount an offensive up the Hudson to Albany.

Burgoyne remained on the Hudson gathering supplies for the final offensive since he realized that he would have to abandon his lines of communication and supply once he started forward because of his lacking the manpower to keep them open in hostile country. On September 13, he moved out with about 5,000 men for the final push to Albany.

On August 1, the Continental Congress had made another of a long line of damaging intrusions into the operations of the army, replacing the capable Schuyler with the incapable General Horatio Gates who had, however, political influence.

On September 12, the Americans, numbering about 12,000, occupied Bemis Heights on the Hudson south of Saratoga and about 25 miles north of Albany, there to await Burgoyne's attack. Yielding the initiative to a numerically inferior enemy can

John Jay: The Forgotten Founder

be justified if plans have been made for going over to the offensive once the assault had been parried. Gates had no such plans.

On September 15, Burgoyne attacked with three columns. Gates remained inactive, taking no steps to bring to bear his superior numbers. Unable to restrain himself, Benedict Arnold, without orders, sprang into his saddle and assumed battlefield command, leading the Americans who had been committed to the fray in a successful counterattack which halted the British in their tracks and threw them back. Unfortunately, Gates did not back Arnold with his uncommitted men and the Americans failed to gain a complete victory. Military historians who have studied the battle believe that had it not been for Arnold's brilliant leadership, the British would have won and reached Albany. Gates, jealous of Arnold, removed him from his command.

On September 24, 3,000 reinforcements from England arrived at New York. Clinton now had 7,000 men under his command, sufficient to hold New York against Washington, whose main force was covering Philadelphia, and to move up the Hudson with 3,000 to aid Burgoyne. By October 5, he was near Peekskill, about 125 miles away.

Another British attack having failed, Burgoyne now had no alternative but to withdraw to the north. Clinton's advance from the south, meeting stiffening American resistance, could not reach him in time. The outnumbered, exhausted British could not make good their escape and, almost surrounded, retreat cut off, they surrendered on October 17.

The brilliant leadership of Arnold, the fighting qualities of the American soldiers, and British mistakes combined to sound the death knell for a sound, dangerous offensive plan which, had it been successful, probably would have led to the military defeat of the American cause.

On November 1, an American ship sailed from Boston across the stormy Atlantic to France where it arrived 30 days later. News of the great American victory electrified the French. On December 6, King Louis XVI approved an alliance with the United States. On February 6, 1778, a formal treaty was signed and on March 11, a state of war existed between France and the United Kingdom. French leaders, still smarting from the British victory in the Seven Years' War (1754-1761), wanted another crack at their old enemies, tearing them down from their position as the most powerful country in the world. Perhaps Canada could be regained and the United States emerge as a French satellite.[18] Silas Deane, the American representative in France, caused problems by giving commissions to too many Frenchmen ill-equipped in everything except an inflated sense of their own military capabilities and of the American need for them. Officers the caliber of Lafayette and de Kalb were all too rare.

The French also plotted to secure the appointment of General Comte de Broglie as commander of the American army. The plan, though, came to naught as the French learned that American determination to be independent of foreign domination was too strong. Initially General Baron de Kalb was one of those who came to these shores intending to push for French command. He, however, came to support Washington and the American cause, stating in a letter to de Broglie that it was "Impossible to succeed in the grand project ... it would be regarded as a crying injustice against Washington and an outrage on the country."[19]

Washington definitely was concerned lest French domination come to replace that of Britain. He foresaw the possibility that France could seize Canada and hold it, that the United States no longer would be an ally useful in reducing British power, but would be regarded as a potential rival to be dominated. These apprehensions he expressed in a letter to Henry Laurens while the latter was serving as president of Congress.[20]

Later the Dutch and the Spanish joined the alliance. The British now faced not just a colonial revolt, but also a major war in several theaters of operation which distracted their attention and resources from North America.

Jay well understood the advantages of the alliance with France, but very much the scion of Huguenots, he had misgivings about the country which had persecuted his ancestors. He had opposed the overbearing British attitude toward the colonies and supported independence, but his political and judicial convictions were much more British than French. Nevertheless he did support the alliance as being beneficial to the cause of American Independence.

With the victory at Saratoga, the tide in the war had turned against the British. Although there were to be times during the remaining four years of conflict when the darkness of defeat would hang over the land, the American sun was rising steadily.

The American main force under Washington, having been defeated at Brandywine on September 9 and almost winning at Germantown on October 5 before a British counterattack gained the battlefield, suffered through the winter of 1777-1778 at Valley Forge, just north of Philadelphia. With the coming of spring and the French alliance, the

British, Clinton having replaced Howe, determined to abandon Philadelphia and concentrate on New York. Washington broke camp at Valley Forge and caught them at Monmouth Courthouse on June 27 where a bitterly fought battle ended in a tactical draw but an American strategic victory as the British continued their retreat to New York. Washington now moved his forces into a semicircle a radius of forty miles out from the city.

The last stage of the war was in the south where there was a substantial Loyalist population. The British plan was to secure Georgia and the Carolinas, then move northward against the primary centers of rebellion. Initially, the strategy worked well. Clinton with General Lord Cornwallis seized Charleston on May 12, 1780. Considering South Carolina under control, the next month Clinton returned to New York leaving Cornwallis in command. Congress, without any input from Washington, now gave Gates command of American forces in the South. He quickly moved against the British contingent at Camden where he was attacked and routed by Cornwallis on August 16, losing most of his equipment and devastating his reputation by precipitously fleeing the battlefield.

General Nathaniel Greene, one of the best American leaders, was selected by Washington to replace Gates, arriving on December 4 to take control of the dispirited American soldiers. This he did successfully, bringing them back into fighting trim. He then divided his command into a number of units operating separately. Cornwallis did the same, one of his segments being defeated at Cowpens by Colonel Daniel Morgan. The main British force under Cornwallis, though, continued its success, defeating Greene on March 15, 1781, at Guilford Court House. Greene, however, kept his army together, was never routed, maintained good morale, replaced his losses, and inflicted losses on the British which they were hard put to replace.

Now, with no viable alternative, Cornwallis moved north into Virginia, establishing himself at Yorktown, a defensible position on a peninsula between the York River and the James River. From this position, he either could receive reinforcements from New York through Chesapeake Bay or be evacuated via the same route. Both prospects were doomed after the naval engagement on September 5 in Chesapeake Bay between the French led by Admiral Count de Grasse and the British commanded by Admiral Thomas Graves. An indecisive battle in which British leadership was not impressive led to the withdrawal of Graves and French control of this key area at this key time.

John Jay: The Forgotten Founder

Meanwhile, Washington had moved the main American army south, masking the operation from Clinton in New York, and accompanied by a French force under General Count de Rochambeau, arrived at Yorktown, confronting Cornwallis with no reasonable alternative to surrender. After some more stiff fighting, he bowed to the inevitable and surrendered on October 17, the fourth anniversary of Burgoyne's capitulation at Saratoga. Two days later, the British marched out to pile arms, their bands playing, "The World Turned Upside Down."

That very day, Clinton sailed from New York with reinforcements. At almost the same time, de Grasse sailed for the West Indies to secure French interests there. Five days too late, Clinton arrived. There was nothing he could do, but return to New York. Although the formal independence of the United States would not be established until the signing of the Treaty of Paris on November 3, 1783, the victory at Yorktown determined that the former thirteen colonies would become a new, free country.

The Life of John Jay

In New York

Jay continued to serve in the Continental Congress until April 1776 when he was elected to the New York Provincial Congress. It is interesting to note that at this time when faced with the necessity to choose between the national Congress and the state body, he returned to New York, his ties to his home state being strong, especially now that the time of the expected British assault drew near and a state constitution had to be drafted. At first, Jay resisted calls for a final break with Britain, but once the Declaration of Independence was passed and the British invasion of New York was imminent, he changed and supported New York's endorsement of independence.

Furthermore, Jay was made chairman of the committee appointed by the New York Provincial Congress to root out pro British activity. The committee was authorized to raise a force of 220 men, apprehend those considered security risks, make drafts on the treasury, and call out the militia in the counties if necessary. Some of these efforts were dramatic, such as quashing a conspiracy involving a few soldiers to become turncoats when the British arrived.[21] Much, however, was more humdrum, yet vital, such as determining who among those not vigorously supporting independence were security threats and who were not. Jay did support a resolution stipulating that anyone living in New York who supported enemies of the state was guilty of treason and, if found guilty, subject to execution. Those, though, who favored the British cause, but did not actively aid them would not be disturbed.

Remember, this was a difficult time when it was easy for subversives to blend in with the population, this being a civil war as well as a conflict against Britain, and execution for treason well could be the price paid by the leaders of the American cause were they to lose. David Matthews, mayor of New York, was found to be subversive and jailed. Jay's close friend, former college mate, and fellow lawyer, Peter Van Schaack, refused to take an oath of allegiance to the new country and was exiled from American territory. After the war ended, their friendship was renewed and Jay sponsored Van Schaack's return to the United States.[22]

Another case involved Beverly Robinson, a man of wealth and social status who lived on an impressive estate on the Hudson River opposite West Point. Having chosen loyalty to the Crown, although initially he attempted to be neutral, on February 22, 1777, he was summoned to appear before Jay's committee meeting at Washington's headquarters at Newburgh. Jay informed him that:

> Sir, we have passed the Rubicon and it is now necessary every man Take his part, Cast off all alliegiance to the King of Great Britain and take an oath of Alliegiance to the States of America or Go over to the Enemy for we have Declared ourselves independent.[23]

To this Robinson responded that he could not take an oath to the United States, but that he wished to remain since his property and goods were in the new country. If forced to leave, he requested that he be permitted to take his effects with him. Jay affirmed that he could, but that the preference was for Robinson to join the cause. He would be given a month or six weeks to decide. In less time than that, he went to New York City, raised and commanded a Loyalist regiment in which four of his sons served, and moved to England after the American victory.[24]

It cannot be determined with any degree of certainty how many people in the new country supported independence (Patriots), how many wished to remain in the British Empire (Loyalists or Tories), and how many desired to stay neutral. Samuel Eliot Morison estimated that about forty percent of the population favored independence, about ten percent were Loyalists, and the remaining half sought to avoid involvement. He went on to say that within the states, Loyalist sentiment ranged from about half of the residents in New York to only ten percent of those in Connecticut.[25]* John Adams considered the proportions to be roughly equal—one third, one third, one third. Joseph Ellis believed about 20 percent supported independence, about fifteen percent were Loyalists, and the rest, by and large, favored whoever was stronger in their area.[26]

Not only would this be a war of rebellion and an international conflict, but also a bitter civil war which tore apart those who had been neighbors; it often was nasty as civil wars tend to be. Often, prisoners were not taken and there were times when they were taken, but then hanged for treason. Loyalists, though, who kept their mouths shut, paid their taxes, and did nothing active to further their convictions generally would be left alone and could remain in their homes.

After the end of the war, most Loyalists remained in the United States or returned there.

---

* Estimates do vary.

However, about 100,000 chose exile instead. A few went to Bermuda, more to the Bahamas and Jamaica, some to England, but the largest number settled in Canada, some 30,000 to Nova Scotia, doubling the population there; others settled in New Brunswick, Ontario, Prince Edward Island, even Quebec.[27] Needless to say, Canada benefited significantly from this influx as did the other New World territories. To this day, people in these places still value their Loyalist roots.

In addition to his counterintelligence activities, Jay also organized and ran a spy ring. He did so by having a militiaman named Enoch Crosby arrested and jailed as a deserter, then arranged his escape into the British lines where he was accepted as a Tory. He proved to be a valuable source of information on British military operations and on Tory recruiting efforts.[28]

Although he had been commissioned a colonel in the New York militia, Jay never assumed an active command position because of his political, judicial, and diplomatic leadership roles. One mission he did undertake was to procure cannons for blocking the Hudson River at West Point. New York had established a powerful Secret Committee to control the Hudson, chaired by Robert Yates and including Jay as a member. The river was part of a vital invasion route. A military force could go by water almost all the way from New York City to the St. Lawrence or the reverse. This route had been attempted by both the British and the French in their previous wars for control of North America and would attract the attention of both sides in the present conflict. Also, were the British to control the Hudson, New England would have been severed from the other parts of the new country.

Jay was:

> Authorized and empowered to impress carriages, teams, sloops, and horses, and to call out detachments of the militia, and generally to do, or cause to be done at his discretion, all such matters and things as he may deem necessary or expedient to forward and complete the business committed to his care.[29]

This Jay did successfully, getting twenty cannons in Salisbury, Connecticut which then were transported to West Point where they aided in blocking the British from gaining total control of the Hudson.

The British military victories on Long Island and Manhattan during the summer of 1776 forced the Provincial Congress to withdraw first to White

Plains, then northward to Poughkeepsie and Kingston. Jay's parents fled the family home in Rye to find refuge with friends in Fishkill.

During this low time in American military status, Jay demonstrated a ruthless streak, advocating a scorched-earth policy—burning New York City to deny the British the use of it as a port and as a base until they expended considerable time, money, and personnel in the rebuilding effort, diverting all these from other uses in the war. His proposal, though, was too draconian and was rejected. Washington evinced support for the idea when, after a fire of a more limited scope destroyed about a fourth of the city just prior to the American evacuation in late September, he remarked that "Providence or some good honest fellow, has done more for us than we were disposed to do for ourselves."[30] He went on to state that, sadly, enough of the city remained to benefit the British substantially.

Meanwhile, in August, a committee chaired by Jay was formed to draft a state constitution. A few days before the finalization of the document in the spring of 1777, he left because his mother was dying. Although in general it represented his convictions, he was disappointed that there was not sufficient support to prohibit slavery. Years later, as governor, Jay took the lead in correcting this. It should be noted that New York did provide for freeing slaves who served in the armed forces and in 1785 forbade the sale of Negroes or others brought into the state.

Jay opposed slavery in principle and called for its gradual abolition. He wanted the slaves to be prepared for freedom so that there would be no societal disruption from the sudden freeing of a mass of people unprepared for the handling of their new situation. The overall population was growing rapidly, the 1790 census reporting 3,929,827. By 1800, it had increased to 5,308,483.[31] Of this total, close to one-fifth were slaves. Illustrative of his growing opposition to slavery and of his belief in gradual emancipation was his involvement with a slave named Benoit, purchased by him in Martinique in 1779. Stopping on the island while on his way to Spain, Jay was impressed by the fifteen year old slave and determined to use him as a personal attendant. In 1784, while serving in Paris, Jay gave Benoit a "conditional manumission" which provided for his freedom after three more years of service.[32] This represented a definite change since the Jay family had held slaves both for household labor and for work in the fields.

Another battle which Jay won was his effort to include in the state constitution a provision stipulating that everyone who held office in New

York must swear allegiance to the government and "renounce all allegiance and subjection to foreign kings, princes, and states, in all matters, ecclesiastical as well as civil."[33] This, of course, was aimed at Roman Catholics who would have had to choose between the pope, who then as well as now is both a head of state and a spiritual leader, and their New York citizenship. This position of his reflected the Jay family background of suffering the loss of freedom and property in the France of Louis XIV following the revocation of the Edict of Nantes. By and large, Jay exhibited religious toleration, but concerning the papacy and its control of the Roman Catholic Church throughout the world, Jay was adamantly in opposition, seeing a clear contradiction with the freedom he valued.

The new state constitution did reflect the principles held by Jay and John Adams that the best government would combine aspects of the monarchial, the aristocratic, and the democratic, namely a chief executive with real power, a legislative house representing the most successful, the most productive, the best educated; and a legislative chamber representing the bulk of the populace.

The power of the governor was restricted in two significant ways, demonstrating the opposition to executive authority which was gaining strength as the rejection of British heavy-handedness grew: appointments were to be made by a Council of Appointment and the veto was shared with a Council of Revision.

With the New York Constitution in effect as of April 20, 1777, Jay was named chief justice of the Supreme Court. In September, he opened the first session in Kingston, up the Hudson River a bit over half way from New York City to Albany. Then, in 1778, he presided over two Supreme Court sessions and two special criminal courts. In addition, he engaged in reviewing legislation.

Here he would not long remain, however; once again the national scene would beckon as the need for the newly independent country to establish an effective government grew and once again Jay would be named a delegate to Congress, returning to Philadelphia in December 1778. This he had been urged to do by his friend, Gouverneur Morris.

Meanwhile, John Dickenson chaired a committee charged with drafting a document setting up a national confederation. The proposal was submitted to Congress in July 1776. The original idea was for the states to be represented in Congress proportionate to their population, but the small states blocked implementation. The final decision was that each state would be represented in the unicameral Congress by at least two but no more than seven representatives, but that each state would cast one vote. Congress was authorized to establish executive departments and did so, setting up five: foreign affairs, war, admiralty, finance, and post office.

As a result of their experiences with the British government, though, Congress was not prepared to create a central government with significant power. Congress had no jurisdiction over interstate or foreign commerce. Expenses of the federal government were assessed in proportion to the value of the land within the states, but there was no mechanism to compel payment by them. No federal judiciary was established. Only by unanimous vote of the states could the Articles be amended, something which would prove to be a crippling stipulation.

On November 15, 1777, the Articles were adopted by Congress and submitted to the states for ratification. Because of the reluctance of some states, Virginia and Maryland in particular, to give way on their western land claims, the Articles did not go into effect until March 1, 1781.

The Life of John Jay

President of the Congress

The Congress to which Jay returned in December 1778 was torn by dissension. Patriotic men such as he, dedicated to independence and ordered freedom, served alongside those who could see no further than their own narrow self-interest or their jealous resentment of those more successful than they. In this the Congress was no different from other parliamentary bodies throughout the history of free societies. After all, it is not always the cream which rises to the top; oftentimes the scum does too. Now, though, times were especially perilous. Although the military situation had improved with the victory at Saratoga in October 1777, triumph in the war by no means was certain. British naval strength on the seas and the British army occupation of key locations such as New York, precluded much trade. The continental dollar was declining in value and inflation was worsening. Foreign loans were critical to keep the government going. Yet there were those who saw little of this or cared little as they sought their own advantage.

Washington himself came under attack from petty self-seekers. In November 1777, Congress had appointed General Horatio Gates, commander of the American forces at Saratoga (although Benedict Arnold deserved credit for the win), president of the Board of War. From this position, he maneuvered to bring down Washington with the intent to take his place in command of the American army. Gates, a former British officer, had considerable experience, but his ability and courage did not come close to matching his inflated ego. The scheming came to naught, brought down by support from the public and the army for Washington and by recognition of the pettiness of Gates and his clique. All too often, Congress would prove to be incapable of raising the funds necessary to support the army, but quite capable of unwarranted interference in its operation. Throughout, Jay's relationship with Washington remained solid, his support of the general firm.

 One of the conflicts rending Congress as Jay returned was that between the Lees of Virginia and the Adamses of Massachusetts on one side and Silas Deane of Connecticut and his allies on the other. Deane, an attorney and former member of Congress, had represented the United States in France with a degree of success, securing money and supplies for the war against the British. There were, however, serious charges that he had skimmed off money for himself. Although the accusations were not substantiated positively, there was an unsavory aroma about the whole Deane record. He was combative, self-righteous, opportunistic, and had a reputation for walking a narrow line in business dealings between the ethical and the shady, the legal and the illegal. At this stage, Jay, a friend of Deane's, was supportive of him.

Another complicating factor was the influence in Congress of Conrad Gerard, the French minister to the United States, who was effective in furthering the interests of his country which, outside of defeating Britain, were not always the same as those of this country. Gerard tended to view opposition to Deane as opposition to France.

Also aggravating the situation was a bitter feud between Deane and Arthur Lee of Virginia who had served with him in France. Lee had been the first to accuse Deane of diverting government money into his own pockets. Deane, in turn, accused Lee of being a security risk because of his consorting with a probable British spy.[34] Congress now would be called upon to sort out this mess.

Henry Laurens of South Carolina, then president of Congress, called for a special committee to deal with the Deane allegations. Congress, though, declined to take action on Laurens' proposal. Deane, infuriated, charged Laurens with obstructing consideration of his case. Everything now became public thanks to the publication by the

Pennsylvania Gazette of Deane's attacks. Laurens now, stating that his honor and that of Congress had been impugned, resigned in a huff. Jay, newly returned, had not been a party to all the infighting. He was highly regarded for his ability and integrity. Gerard considered him a friend of France, which he was, although he was an American first and would become suspicious of French intentions beyond their wanting to hurt British interests, a sentiment which would become especially clear when he was a member of the American delegation in Paris negotiating peace.

Furthermore, Jay previously had clashed with Arthur Lee of Virginia who had served in France with Deane and brought the charges against him. As a result of his experiences with Lee, Jay was leery of his veracity and inclined to the Deane side.

Jay's relationship with Deane was subjected to severe stress a few years later after the war had ended. Jay learned of friendly meetings between Deane and Benedict Arnold. Jay, still in France, wrote to Deane that he had "possessed my esteem," that personally he never had been offended by him. But, he continued, "I love my country and my honor better than my friends, and even my family, and am ready to part with them all whenever it would be improper to retain them." Jay went on, writing to Deane that "you are either exceedingly injured, or you are no friend to America; and while doubts remain on that point, all connexion between us must be suspended." He informed Deane that the information concerning his friendly relations with Arnold had come to him from a reliable source. He then commented that "Every American who gives his hand to that man, in my opinion, pollutes it."[35] Even though the war with the British was over and even though Jay was rather an Anglophile deep down, the odious nature of Arnold's having both betrayed his country and then waged war against it, made acceptance of Arnold and of anyone befriending him absolutely unacceptable, from Jay's perspective, for any true American. Honor and propriety always loomed large with him coming before more personal considerations.

Nothing definitive has been found pointing either to Deane's innocence or to his guilt; in 1789 he died, a derelict, cause unknown.

As a result of all this, just a matter of days after his return to Congress, Jay was elected president of the body. The powers of this office were limited. As president, Jay did not have the authority to determine the business to be undertaken by Congress, nor could he control committee membership. Furthermore, there was a pattern that each president would serve only about one year. Still, though, he did as much as could have been done to strengthen the country, being effective in supporting Washington against his detractors and keeping the focus on prosecuting the war. He was to handle well the frustrations of holding a position with considerable responsibilities but with little power to determine the course of events.

Finances were a major concern. Jay viewed with consternation the depreciation of the dollar and the decline of confidence in American government bonds both at home and abroad. He issued a statement that debts contracted by government had to be honored if national integrity were to be established, a position foreshadowing Alexander Hamilton's later stance as secretary of the treasury. Further, he admonished the states to pay their taxes and called for the abandonment of monetary inflation as the way to finance government. Taxes and loans, troubling though they may be, were less dangerous.

Congress on September 8, 1779 adopted a circular letter to the states written by Jay. Even though the Articles of Confederation at that time were one state short of ratification, the states were informed that as a practical matter, the confederation was an accomplished fact. He cited the instructions given to the First and Second Congresses and the Declaration of Independence.[36]

Consistently he affirmed that Congress was superior to the states in matters of war and peace, that it was sovereign in these matters. Of Jay, Richard B. Morris stated that "Jay's presidency of Congress marked the zenith of presidential activism during the years of the Continental Congress."[37]

Later in September, it became clear that a new need had arisen for Jay's talents; Congress chose him for what was considered a post more vital to the war effort, minister to Spain. Here again political machinations intruded in the choice. Arthur Lee desired the posting, but his attacks on Deane had antagonized a number of congressmen. Also, when John Adams was selected as the American peace commissioner, there were middle states congressmen who believed Jay should have received the posting.[38] These factors helped convince most members of Congress that Jay was the best man for Madrid, but, overall, his stature was the key consideration.

The Life of John Jay

Spain

On October 20, 1779, Jay and his party sailed from Philadelphia on the frigate U.S.S. Confederacy. Accompanying him were his wife, secretary of legation William Carmichael, and his personal secretary and brother-in-law Henry Brockholst Livingston. Also traveling with them was Conrad Gerard, the former French minister who was returning home.

The voyage turned out to be more of an adventure than they wanted. A fierce storm hit the ship on November 7, bringing down all three masts and knocking out the rudder. With a jury-rigged mast and improvised rudder, continuing to France was out of the question and the Confederacy slowly, laboriously made her way to Martinique in the French West Indies. Providentially, no British warships sighted them. An encounter with the Confederacy in this condition would have been disastrous; she could have been destroyed at leisure or forced to strike her colors. From Martinique, the Jay party sailed on the French frigate Aurora for Cadiz, landing on January 22, 1780. Originally, Jay's intention had been to sail on into the Mediterranean to Toulon in the south of France, then travel to Paris for a conference with Franklin before taking up his duties in Spain. In Cadiz, however, he learned that the British had defeated the Spanish navy, making his odds of reaching Toulon by sea rather slim. After a slow, arduous journey, they arrived in Madrid in April where Jay now entered into the most frustrating of all the tasks he had undertaken for his country.

Jay's mission was to secure Spanish recognition of American independence and financial aid. Spain was willing, grudgingly, to part with some money, but recognition of the United States was out of the question. King Carlos III and Prime Minister Conde (Count) de Floridablanca had no desire to see a republic come into existence in the New World where their own colonies already were becoming restive. Their interest in the United States existed only in terms of furthering Spanish interests. Not only did Floridablanca have no use for republics, but he also did not like France and, therefore, the prospect of an alliance with that country. Before Jay was not the easiest of diplomatic assignments!

France, also furthering its own interests, had negotiated with Spain to secure an alliance against the British. This was agreed to after several provisos were met. First, the British had to reject a Spanish proposal for an international conference to mediate the war with the American colonies. This happened since Britain was not about to let other countries meddle in its business. Second, France agreed to continue the war until Spain had regained Gibraltar and East and West Florida. Additionally, France would protect Spanish interests against American expansionism.[39]

Spain, once the greatest power in the Western World, had been declining for a couple of centuries. Its naval strength had been slipping since the British won the Spanish Armada campaign in 1588 and its once dominant army had lost that position after being superseded by the French during the next century; Spain's long, slow decline had begun. Although fading as a continental power, Spain did intend to maintain, even augment its colonial empire. This meant weakening Britain which necessitated accepting American independence and allying itself with France, distinctly unpleasant prospects, but unavoidable. Spain was determined to regain Gibraltar, Minorca, and Florida, to conquer Portugal, and to control the Mississippi River Valley and the Gulf of Mexico. Fear of westward American expansion led to Spanish schemes to control the territory north of the settled areas of Mexico. The French secretly supported Spanish intentions to check American expansion by controlling the Mississippi and Florida.[40]

For all these reasons, Jay's mission was doomed from the start. The Spanish government had to accept the reality that the American colonies would become an independent country, but rather petulantly they refused to accept officially Jay as a minister plenipotentiary and King Carlos III never received him, although Prime Minister Floridablanca did meet with him. Spanish financial aid was a mere pittance.

To exacerbate his problems, Jay had a troublesome staff. William Carmichael, secretary of legation, turned out to be self-centered, careless with his finances, and disrespectful to Jay. These characteristics led to a serious rift between the two men. Henry Brockholst Livingston, Jay's personal secretary and brother-in-law, had served as a colonel in the army, but there was little else good to say of him. Richard Morris described him as "captious, sulky, ill-mannered, and thoroughly spoiled."[41] Clashing with both Jay and his sister, he soon departed for home. The third problem was Lewis Littlepage, a young Virginian who came to Madrid with the recommendation of a friend of Jay's in that state. The Jays provided a home for him, but he showed little interest in diplomacy, much preferring war and women. He left his post to join the Spanish army in combat against the British at Gibraltar.

Finally, during his time in Spain, Jay had numerous health problems—influenza, rheumatism, dysentery and other digestive system difficulties, throat problems, and a "pain in the breast" not otherwise explained. No doubt all the turmoil contributed to these maladies.

Still, during the two years Jay spent in Spain, he did as well as was possible with the poor hand he had been dealt. An end was coming, though, to Jay's ordeal.

During this period, the French were considering a settlement with the British which would not guarantee American independence. To clear the way, Foreign Minister Vergennes instructed La Luzerne, the ambassador to the United States, to get John Adams removed as the sole American peacemaker. La Luzerne pushed hard, using his influence in Congress as the representative of our most powerful ally plus bribing some members. Congress was split, partially in terms of their opinion of Adams, partially on how much they trusted France, partially concerning how much they believed we had to kowtow to France. La Luzerne called for an American diplomatic agent pledged to "take no steps without the approbation of his Majesty," and that this man would "receive his directions from the Comte de Vergennes."[42]

In June 1781, Congress agreed to most of the French demands. Adams was not removed, but now would be one of five commissioners, each from a different region: Adams, New England; John Jay, New York; Benjamin Franklin, Pennsylvania; Thomas Jefferson, Virginia; and Henry Laurens, South Carolina. At the time, Adams was in the Netherlands, Jay in Spain, and Franklin in France. Jefferson declined the position, preferring to remain in Virginia. Laurens was in the Tower of London, having been captured by a British Naval ship while on his way to the Netherlands. So off Jay went to Paris.

The Treaty of Paris

The British defeat at Yorktown in October 1781 doomed Lord North's ministry which had proven unable either to win the war militarily or to negotiate an acceptable settlement. They still held significant locations such as New York, Charleston, and forts on the northern frontier, but it was clear that the war could not be won, especially with France, Spain, and the Netherlands also as enemies. North understood reality, but George III resisted until March 1782 when he accepted North's resignation and the Marquess of Rockingham, who had served as prime minister back in 1765-1766, replaced him. Rockingham and his Whigs, although patriotic Britishers, had opposed the harsh treatment of the colonists before the war and now were prepared to accept that the North American colonies were an independent country and that Britain could not subjugate them plus fight France, Spain, and the Netherlands. The Earl of Shelburne became home secretary, succeeding to the prime ministership in July following the death of Rockingham.

Meanwhile, Jay had remained in Spain, still hoping that he could further American interests. Now, though, the change in British administrations meant that serious negotiations would begin; on June 23 1782, he arrived in Paris. During most of the following month, an attack of influenza had him out of commission. Almost at the time Jay returned to duty, Franklin was rendered *hors de combat* by gout and kidney stones. For several weeks, until Franklin recovered and Adams arrived in October having secured Dutch recognition of the United States and a treaty of commerce, Jay was the sole American diplomat meeting with Richard Oswald who represented the British government.

Jay, though, refused to engage in formal talks until the British recognized the United States as an independent country. Jay asserted that his country had designated itself "the United States of America," whereas Oswald's commission authorized him "to conclude a peace or truce with certain Colonies in North America."[43] He went on, stating that:

> Nations, particularly corporations, mercantile companies, and indeed every private citizen, in every country, have their titles, their styles, their firms, and their additions, which are necessary to their being known in the law; that is to say, the law of nations requires

> that national acts shall give to every sovereign and nation its proper political name or style, in the same manner as the municipal law of the land will only take notice of corporations, companies, and even private citizens by their proper names and legal descriptions.[44]

Jay continued, averring that:

> Mr. Oswald's commission is a formal, national act, and no nation not mentioned or properly described in it can consider him properly authorized to treat with them. Neither the United States of America, nor Commissioners appointed by them, are mentioned in it, and therefore we as their servants can have no right to treat with him.[45]

In his recent biography of Jay, Walter Stahr wrote that he regarded this stance on Jay's part as excessive, that he was being stubbornly legalistic: "On balance, although one can admire Jay's patriotism in wanting to see early recognition of America's status, one has to question his judgment in insisting that this be dealt with as a precondition."[46] Jonathan Dull also considered Jay out of line, that his insistence on this point needlessly delayed settlement of the war.[47]

Vergennes too disagreed, arguing that the talks should go on with recognition of independence something to be part of the treaty. Jay won the point, thanks to the British government's desire to end the war with the Americans and, hopefully, to separate them from the French plus the fact that Oswald was favorably inclined toward the United States. Since the British ended up accepting Jay's demand, even though negotiations were delayed for two months, it is hard to fault him for his stalwart defense of this country's status. It certainly could be argued that this stance so impressed the British with American determination that it led to a quicker resolution than otherwise would have happened.

Interestingly, British secret service reports, while acknowledging his courage, zeal, and gifts as a speaker and as a writer, also described him as "naturally controversial" and obstinate. Touchiness and vanity also were attributed to him.[48] These characterizations were by no means devoid of validity, but they were controlled by him and did not detract from his success as a diplomat, as chief justice of the Supreme Court, or as governor of New York.

John Jay: The Forgotten Founder

At the same time, Vergennes was playing a double game, secretly sending word to Shelburne that France did not support all the American positions. Although Vergennes was friendly to the United States, now that the war for American independence had been won and British power somewhat reduced, it was time to further French interests which did not include having the new country get too powerful. Jay and Adams suspected the French of shenanigans and were prepared to negotiate with the British directly in spite of treaty stipulations that the United States and France would act together. A rather Byzantine scene now would ensue with the three countries each attemptting to further its interests.

Each of the three delegates was a committed patriot and a man of outstanding intellect and ability. They were, though, substantially different in religious convictions, views of France, and in personality. Spiritually they ranged from Jay, an evangelical Christian, to Franklin, a believer in God, but overall a man of the Enlightenment who was unconcerned about questions relating to the deity of Christ, rejected the Trinity, and did not accept the Bible as divine revelation. Adams was between them; he was deeply religious, read the Bible faithfully, but was Unitarian. Franklin was, as a man of the Enlightenment, pro French and very much at home in the salons of Paris. Jay, the firm Christian and descendent of Huguenots, was not. He and Adams were suspicious of French intentions, seeing France as willing to be allied with us to reduce British power, but not supportive of a strong United States, particularly one expanding westward. A skilled diplomat fully recognizing the need for French aid, Jay, though, was convinced that the United States must exercise great care when dealing with France. Presently the alliance was beneficial to both parties, but the long-term interests of the two countries were not the same. He argued that:

> We can depend upon the French only to see that we are separated from England, but it is not in their interest that we should become a great and formidable people, and therefore they will not help us become so.[49]

In terms of temperament, Franklin was relaxed and convivial, Jay rather the aloof aristocrat, except in private, and Adams the flinty, crusty New Englander. The American diplomats recognized that neither Britain nor France was enthusiastic about an independent, prosperous, and strong United States. But, the two were enemies; each wished to weaken the other, so there were good cards for the Americans to play. The British had to recognize the reality that the American colonies were gone. They did not want to drive them totally into the arms of France by being too intransigent; it was in the British interest to make the best of a bad situation. This would happen, British opinion in general lamenting the policy blunders that drove the colonies into rebellion, but also lamenting that they now were independent. Some subjects of King George were bitter and wanted to strike at the new country by holding on to forts in the Great Lakes region and supporting Indian opposition to westward expansion by Americans.

Henry Strachey was added to the British delegation in order to stiffen the stances taken by the more compliant Oswald. Of the two delegations, David McCullough wrote:

> In fact, the British envoys were not particularly impressive. In ability, experience, and resolve they were hardly a match for Adams, Franklin, and Jay, who, having started from scratch as diplomats, had come a long way in their time in Europe.[50]

The Life of John Jay

Formal discussions between the two sides got under way on October 30. For a month, they debated the borders the United States would have, use of the Mississippi, payment due British business interests by Americans, compensation of Loyalists, and American fishing rights on the Grand Banks. Jay and Franklin opposed paying the British merchants what was owed them, believing that British destruction and confiscation of American property more than equaled the debts. Adams, though, insisted that as a matter of honor and legality, the debts must be paid. This was agreed to, but not much came of it.

Late in November, Henry Laurens joined the other peace commissioners, having been exchanged for General Cornwallis. He, though, was close to being a broken man, the result of his health being damaged by imprisonment and the death of his son in a minor skirmish with the British months after Yorktown.

On November 30, a preliminary treaty was signed in Oswald's quarters at the Grand Hotel Moscovite in Paris. The United States gained the territory extending from the Appalachian Mountains to the Mississippi River. The country now would extend from Canada to Florida and from the Atlantic to the Mississippi. Use of the Mississippi was open to both American and British subjects.

John Jay: The Forgotten Founder

The British did agree to American fishing rights on the Grand Banks and Americans could land to cure fish in unpopulated areas. They also agreed to withdraw their armed forces from what was to be American territory. The Loyalists were promised nothing in the treaty, although the Americans did agree to request that the states do something. Not too surprisingly, this did not amount to anything.

Technically, the American negotiators had acted contrary to the orders of Congress that Vergennes' advice was to be followed and that the French were to be involved in the treaty. Yet, they believed that the circumstances, given such slow communication at the time, warranted what they did. The first step was to smooth things over with the French. This was assigned to Franklin, the man with the best relations with them. Vergennes was unhappy that the negotiations had been bilateral, but responded affirmatively to Franklin's argument that nothing be permitted to drive a wedge between the United States and France, that were that to happen, it would benefit British interests.

Presented with a very favorable treaty, Congress did the logical thing and ratified it. On September 3, 1783, the Treaty of Paris was signed officially at the Hotel d'York. David Hartley now represented the British government. Laurens having returned home, Jay, Adams, and Franklin signed for the United States. The new country had been well served by these extraordinary men, men of honor, intelligence and courage. Of them, Richard B. Morris said:

> What was so remarkable about the achievements of the American commissioners was that where they compromised it was on inessentials and where they conceded it was to yield the trivial. From beginning to end they remained unswerving on the score of obtaining both absolute independence and a continental domain for thirteen littoral states. On the main objectives of national survival they proved uncompromising. Because the American commissioners resolutely contended for the right of a sovereign people to choose their own form of government... a free people is eternally in their debt.[51]

The Jays remained in France until the spring of 1784. On May 16, they left Paris. It was Jay's intention to retire from public life and return to his law practice in New York. But, for a man of his stature, so widely respected, private life was a good many years in the future. While his ship still was sailing across the Atlantic, Congress elected him secretary for foreign affairs.

The Life of John Jay

Secretary for Foreign Affairs

Upon his return to the United States, Jay hesitated before agreeing to accept this new office. Partially, he was attracted by the prospect of returning to private life now that war was over, but also he recognized the weakness of the central government under the Articles of Confederation, that this, combined with our weak armed forces, would result in his holding a weak hand when dealing with other countries. Appeals to his sense of duty won and he was sworn in on December 21, 1784. He would remain in the position for five years until the Constitution came into effect.

Commenting upon Jay, the usually sound and perceptive Forrest McDonald managed within a single sentence to compliment Jay, deflate the praise, and insult him:

> John Jay, a brilliant and almost pathologically honest New York aristocrat, a dedicated nationalist and also a pompous and pathetically vain man, was Congress' secretary for foreign affairs.[52]

Certainly he was brilliant and a dedicated nationalist. Pompous he may have been on occasions, but "pathetically vain" clearly is beyond the pale. Furthermore, to refer to someone as "almost pathologically honest" is somewhere in the twilight zone between expressing admiration for him and calling him demented.

Supporters of Jay shortly thereafter urged him to run for the governorship of New York. He, however, considered himself obligated to serve in the office for which he only recently had been selected. In a letter to General Philip Schuyler written June 10, 1785, he stated this point, adding that if New York were facing serious threats, he would think differently, but, that not being the situation, the call of Congress must take precedence.[53]

The United States now faced some serious complexities in its foreign policy. No longer would Britain as the enemy attract to this country allies who wanted to attack the common foe. Now Spain and France had interests which ran counter to ours and even though we and Britain now were at peace, by no means was everything amicable. Most Loyalists settled in as Americans, but the bitterness of some who went into exile was exacerbated by their inability to collect compensation from some states for confiscated property. Also, prewar debts contracted by Americans were not all honored.

Furthermore, the British refused to evacuate seven forts. They did remove themselves from positions they held on the Atlantic coast, but continued to occupy posts in the north—on Lake Champlain plus Ogdensburg, Oswego, Niagara, Detroit, and Michilimackinac. Initially, the British dragged their heels because of the lucrative fur trade. They also were interested in friendly relations with Indians, in particular the Iroquois Confederacy, as a check on American expansion into the region. Finally, the American refusal to pay the debts fully and complaints over treatment of the Loyalists provided justification for staying put.

Spain too would be a serious challenge for Jay. Back in 1780-1781, when he had been minister plenipotentiary to that country, he had angered them by refusing to abandon American insistence on free navigation of the Mississippi. Although the Spanish attempt to recapture Gibraltar failed, they did regain Florida as a result of the war and stationed military forces at Natchez and the present site of Vicksburg, disputing the right of Britain to cede to the United States the eastern side of the Mississippi. Spain was determined keep the area west of the Mississippi free from American expansion, preserving it as a buffer zone protecting Mexico and its great wealth. Loyalists in Pensacola supplied war material to Indians, especially the Creeks, Choctaws, and Cherokees who had allied themselves with the Spanish against the Americans. Raiding of American settlements on the Cumberland and Tennessee Rivers broke out. Spain sent Diego de Gardoqui, with whom Jay had crossed swords during his time in that country, to serve as chargé d'affaires in the United States.

Jay was not enthusiastic about a too rapid development of the West lest national unity be weakened, that centrifugal forces could lead to a sundering of the country. By no means was he alone in this uneasiness. George Washington and James Monroe, among others, expressed concern that the bonds of national unity could be lessened. He further believed that the interests of the Atlantic coast states could be damaged by a westward shift in the national center of gravity. A final very grave worry was that if conflict were to develop with Spain, that France would take its side, a situation we had to avoid.

Jay was prepared to defer—not abandon—American claims to usage of the Mississippi for twenty-five years in return for a treaty opening Spanish colonies to American trade. In fact, seven northern states, focusing more on trade than on freedom to use the Mississippi, voted to instruct him to yield on access to the river for twenty-five or thirty years in return for the opening of Spanish markets. Jay believed that our need for the river would not be great until those years had elapsed and that time was on our side. As the United States grew and developed with the passage of the years, we would be better able to assert our rights.

Theodore Roosevelt, known primarily as a man of action who exuded dynamism, courage, and integrity, which he certainly was, also was a man of letters, an accomplished historian. In *The Winning of the West*, he wrote of Jay's negotiations with Gardoqui, stating that Jay, like many other leaders of the day, did not realize how rapidly Kentucky had grown and underestimated how soon navigation of the Mississippi would be needed by Americans in the region. Although he very much admired him, Roosevelt did concede that "Jay showed less than his usual far-sightedness in this matter...."[54]

After extensive wrangling, Jay attempted a compromise settlement. For now, the United States would drop its claim to usage of the Mississippi in return for a treaty opening Spanish colonies to American trade. When this proposal came before Congress, Jay was attacked by westerners for having abandoned their interests—they needed the

Mississippi to get their products to market—in order to benefit traders on the Atlantic coast. Actually, considering the political and military weakness of the United States, he made the best deal he could, but opposition was so vehement that Congress tabled the matter.

He did succeed in blocking a 1785 consular convention with France which would have given far more advantage to French citizens in this country than the reverse. Jay persuaded Congress to reject ratification. In 1788, an agreement fair and equitable to both sides was concluded. Among other constructive contributions made by Jay during his time in office were the establishment of the consular service, initially with consuls in nineteen foreign ports, and the opening of trade with China.

The United States, an increasingly successful merchant power with a weak navy, was a prime target for the North African Barbary states.* Even though tribute was paid, still American ships and citizens were seized. Sadly and embarrassingly, the American navy was too weak at the time to protect

---

* Muslim Arab armies had swept aside the Byzantines and surged across North Africa during the middle and latter years of the seventh century, supplanting Christian civilization. In the late eighteenth century, the Barbary states (Morocco, Algeria, Tunisia, and Tripoli) were virtually independent countries, technically under Turkish suzerainty.

material honor or the lives and freedom of our citizens. In addition, the government was too poor to ransom captives as a regular practice and the states were reluctant to provide funds from their coffers. As might have been anticipated, this weak attitude engendered more aggression until corrective action became the only course for an honorable and strong people. At one stage in 1785, Algeria actually declared war on the United States. Jay hoped that this would jolt the Americans out of their lethargy and lead to a stronger central government and a stronger navy. He stated that:

> This war does not strike me as a great evil. The more we are ill-treated abroad the more we shall unite and consolidate at home. Besides, as it may become a nursery for seamen, and lay the foundation for a respectable navy, it may prove more beneficial than otherwise.[55]

His observations certainly were true, but would not come to fruition until early in the next century when this country finally acted to eliminate the Barbary threat. We defeated Tripoli in the war of 1801-1805 and Algeria in 1815.

When Jay called for the British to remove their forces from American soil, they refused, admitting that their remaining was contrary to the Treaty of Paris, but accusing the Americans with violating the article that called for creditors on both sides to be able to collect debts without facing impediments. Jay testified before Congress that the British started the trouble by carrying off slaves who had fled their masters for the British lines during the late war. The antislavery Jay supported the retention of freedom by the former slaves, but argued that the British, because of a treaty article forbidding the removal of slaves from the United States, should compensate the former masters. The British refusal to do so warranted obstructing their collecting pre-war debts. He proposed that all states repeal laws interfering with the treaty, that we admit having violated the treaty, that the British government compensate the former slave masters, and that they withdraw from the forts.[56]

During his tenure as secretary for foreign affairs, Jay did all that could have been expected handling the foreign policy of a country with extensive territory, unfriendly neighbors, and weak armed forces. Furthermore, the central government under the Articles of Confederation was incapable of governing. Many Americans had to relearn what Jay, Washington, Hamilton, John

John Jay: The Forgotten Founder

Adams and the other key leaders knew, namely that weak countries do not get left alone; they invite aggression. Jay now would be in the forefront of those calling for their fellow citizens to learn from the mistakes of the Articles and move on to something better.

The Life of John Jay

The Constitution

The Articles of Confederation proved to be inadequate to the task of providing a successful government for the new country. As happens so often, most American political leaders overreacted to their experiences with arbitrary British rule and brought in the opposite—government too weak for civic health. Now the balance had to be redressed.

On a number of occasions, Washington had expressed his concerns. On August 15, 1786, he wrote to Jay, stating his recognition of the need for change and his understanding of the human sin nature:

> We have errors to correct. We have probably had too good an opinion of human nature in forming our confederation. Experience has taught us, that men will not adopt and carry into execution, measures the best calculated for their own good without the intervention of a coercive power. I do not conceive we can exist long as a nation, without having lodged somewhere a power which will pervade the

whole Union in as energetic a manner, as the authority of the different state governments extends over the several States.[57]

Several months later, he again commented to the same effect, writing to Jay on March 10, 1787, a few weeks after Congress had issued the call for a national convention. In it, he stated that:

> Among men of reflection few will be found I believe, who are not beginning to think that our system is better in theory than practice—and that, notwithstanding the boasted virtue of America it is more than probable we shall exhibit the last melancholy proof that mankind are not competent to their own government without the means of coercion in the Sovereign.[58]

Since the national government did not control interstate commerce, states placed barriers on each others' trade. Virginia called for a conference to deal with these problems. It convened in Annapolis, Maryland in September 1786, attended by delegates from only five states. Realizing that nothing substantial could be accomplished with representation from so few states, the delegates at Annapolis, in particular Alexander Hamilton and James Madison, stated the need for a serious national convention. An uprising in late 1786-early 1787 by debtors in western Massachusetts led by Daniel Shays caused alarm among law-abiding, property owning people and increased the demand for a stronger central government. On February 21, 1787, Congress issued the call.

From May 25 to September 17 of that same year, the Constitutional Convention met in Philadelphia, attended by all states except Rhode Island which was controlled by agrarian pro-inflation, anti-specie interests who feared a strong central government would introduce specie and specie backed money. During the typical summer in Philadelphia, heat and humidity commonly press down on those who have not escaped to cooler climes. There were those who said this was the most oppressive summer since 1750. To further exacerbate the situation, in the Pennsylvania State House, now Independence Hall, windows were kept shut to ensure privacy for the deliberations. Even though the building had high ceilings and slatted blinds to shut out the sun, conditions were not pleasant much of the time during summer in Philadelphia in the days before air conditioning.

Most of the prominent national leaders were in attendance with only a few exceptions. Jay was not present due to New York politics. At that time, the state was controlled by George Clinton who opposed the strong nationalism of Jay, Hamilton, and Philip Schuyler. Schuyler, Hamilton's father-in-law, worked out a compromise with Clinton which resulted in Hamilton's election as a delegate, checked, though, by Robert Lansing and John Yates, both Clinton loyalists. Hamilton tried to get two more men added to the New York delegation, Jay being his first choice, but he failed and the Clinton/Schuyler arrangement remained in place.[59]

John Adams and Thomas Jefferson were on diplomatic assignments in Europe, Adams as envoy to Britain, Jefferson to France. Samuel Adams was not selected by Massachusetts and Patrick Henry decided against attending. The latter two opposed strong central government. The fifty-five delegates were mostly young in years. At eighty-one, Benjamin Franklin was the oldest by a margin of fifteen years. In addition to him, only three other men were older than sixty and five were under thirty.

The stature of the fifty-five men responsible for the Constitution has been little disputed; during few times in history can there be found such an array of capable and highly principled leaders. Of them Joseph Ellis wrote that "They comprised by any informed and fair-minded standard, the greatest generation of political talent in American history."[60] While their historical knowledge, political wisdom, and civic mindedness are widely respected, there is more controversy concerning their Christianity. A Christian world view was evident in their thought, but how deep and how extensive was their Christian belief?

They, along with their fellow Americans, had been influenced in varying degrees by both the First Great Awakening and the Enlightenment. The first, a Christian revival movement, swept through the colonies during the 1740s and 1750s. This movement is most associated with the Congregationalist Jonathan Edwards of Massachusetts, a great theologian and a great preacher, and the Englishmen George Whitefield of the Church of England who vigorously traveled through the colonies bringing the message of salvation through Christ and Christian living to crowds of as many as 8,000. Also of significance were the Presbyterians Gilbert Tennant and Samuel Davies and the Baptists Shubal Stearns and Daniel Marshall. Not only did many people accept Christ as Savior and Lord and amend their lives, but also strengthened were the love of freedom from oppression, the conviction that arbitrary, unchecked power, whether ecclesiastical or political, is dangerous, and the belief that social status does not determine human worth. There were some excesses of emotionalism and some took the renewed emphasis on a personal relationship with God to the extreme of denigrating the church as an institution, but overall the First Great Awakening was a positive force.

The Enlightenment developed during the seventeenth century, but peaked in the eighteenth century with which it generally is associated. It rejected the Bible as divine revelation and proclaimed human reason as the highest authority; only those parts of the Bible which survived the test of reason were kept. Education, especially higher education, both in the colonies and in Europe, was impacted substantially.

The rationalism of the English colonists, though, was more that of the Scottish rationalists such as John Locke, Adam Smith, and David Hume rather than that of French thinkers such as Voltaire. The significance is that the Scots still had a vestige of Calvinistic beliefs in that they were dubious about human perfectibility and believed in limited government.

Concerning the beliefs of the founders, Russell Kirk asserted that at least fifty of the fifty-five would have subscribed to the Apostle's Creed, although, because of the gentleman's code to which they adhered, most would not have been religiously demonstrative.[61]

John Eidsmoe maintained that the majority of the delegates to the Constitutional Convention had expressed their adherence to Christian doctrine. He said:

> First, few if any of the fifty-five delegates to the convention identified themselves with deism. Dr. M. E. Bradford catalogs only three as deists (Benjamin Franklin, Hugh Williamson, and James Wilson). I question even these. Of the rest, there were twenty-eight Episcopalians, eight Presbyterians, seven Congregationists, two Lutherans, two Reformed, two Methodists, and two Roman Catholics (one delegate's religious preference cannot be determined). Church membership was not a mere formality among the Founding Fathers. Most were faithful in church attendance, and of these many held church office.[62]

In the Constitution, though, no mention of God is to be found. There are those who do not regard that omission as significant. Pat Robertson, for example, wrote: "That Constitution, as our man-made plan for government, is not an appropriate or necessary place to speak of God. The Declaration had said enough."[63] Clarence Carson also set forth the same conclusion, writing that the decision by the Founding Fathers to leave out of the Constitution any Christian foundation statement did not mean, in most cases, that they were not believers. They believed that Christian precepts undergirded the government they established, but that the enunciation of these precepts should not be made by the government.[64]

Certainly those who wrote the colonial charters believed that foundational political documents were the appropriate places for Christians to affirm their belief in the sovereignty of God and devotion to Christianity. As for the references to God in the Declaration of Independence, they are general in nature, theistic at best, not specifically Christian.

Rousas Rushdoony commented that:

When reference is made to the Christian nature of the United States, the objection immediately raised is the

> absence of reference to Christianity in the Constitution. The Constitution would never have been ratified had such reference been made....[65]

Rushdoony's point was that opposition to a national state church lay behind this aversion. It would appear more likely, however, that this omission was indicative of a weakening of Christian convictions. Even if Rushdoony's contention were true, such a fear was no justification for not even trying.

Mark Noll considered some of these men, such as Roger Sherman, to have been evangelical, but did not so regard many of them. "Most of the leading founders were sincerely religious persons. At the same time, the most influential of their number practiced decidedly nontraditional forms of Christianity."[66] Thomas Jefferson exemplified this nontraditionalism.

Harold O. J. Brown, expressing greater concerns, stated of our early national leaders:

> ... they were more deistic than Christian. In light of the fact that people of non-Christian background, i.e., Jews, were a minuscule minority in the original Colonies and the new States,

we have to recognize in the Founding Fathers' scrupulous avoidance of reference to Christ more than a mere expression of tact towards non-Christians. Between the early colonial charters and compacts that explicitly mention the Christian faith and speak of Jesus Christ as the Lord and Saviour of the world, and the Declaration of Independence, there is a marked difference.[67]

James Madison, for example, while believing that a "high Providence" directed the course of human events, had been influenced by Enlightenment rationalism to such an extent that he rejected the Divine inspiration of the Bible.[68]

George Washington, who presided over the Constitutional Convention and served as the first president under the new Constitution, was the obvious choice for both positions. He was a man of impressive physical mien who had a natural dignity and a palpable sense of leadership evident to all who came into contact with him. His integrity and sound judgment were respected widely. His keen grasp of history added another dimension to his qualities of greatness. So manifest were all these than no challenge to him was possible.

Washington's spiritual faith is disputed with some regarding him as a firm Christian, others classifying him as one who reflected Enlightenment religious views. Although not as clearly a practicing Christian as John Jay, Roger Sherman, John Witherspoon, or Patrick Henry, Washington probably was a believer.

Peter Marshall and David Manuel, co-authors of *The Light and the Glory*, are convinced that Washington was a Christian, basing their conviction to a large extent on incidents recorded in a book published in 1919 by William Johnson entitled *George Washington, the Christian*.[69]

Although carefully considering matters such as his sporadic reception of Holy Communion and his not having testified clearly concerning his faith, John Eidsmoe concluded that Washington was a Christian, that what can be gleaned from what he did say and what others said of him warranted this judgment.[70] Eidsmoe cited a twenty-four page hand-written collection of prayers discovered in 1891 among Washington's papers. There are references to Christ as Savior and Lord and to His atoning death on the Cross in these prayers. Scholars have not determined whether he thought them up or copied them. At any rate, the fact that he valued these prayers sufficiently to write them down and to keep them is significant.[71]

Gary North too referred to Washington's hand-written prayer book and to the specific Christian aspects of it, but he was more concerned with Washington's having been a Mason, with his frequent missing of Holy Communion, and with his public statements being more theistic than clearly Christian. He does concede, though, that Washington may have been a "Christian in private," a "closet Trinitarian."[72]

Most negative in reference to Washington's faith was Francis Rufus Bellamy who stated that Washington lacked a conviction of personal faith, that he was a Deist rather than a Christian.[73]

The best conclusion which can be drawn is that, as was said above, Washington probably believed, albeit unreflectively, in the basic fundamentals of Christianity.

Next to Washington, the most important figure in the first administration was Alexander Hamilton. His life followed a pattern not uncommon in its spiritual course. As a youth, he faithfully followed the forms of Anglican worship, although he did not formally join the church. He entered King's College (later Columbia University) in late 1773 or early 1774. At that time, students there were required to attend Church of England services both morning and evening.[74]

John Jay: The Forgotten Founder

In 1776, Hamilton, twenty-one years of age*, was commissioned as a captain in a New York artillery unit and quickly earned a reputation for ability and courage which gained him a place on Washington's staff. He chafed at staff duty, but was too valuable to be replaced until, finally, he secured a field command again in time for heroic achievement at Yorktown in 1781.

In the early postwar years, he distinguished himself as a brilliant proponent of a strong central government as the best means to preserve order, justice, and freedom. He favored a private sector economy based on manufacturing rather than the Jeffersonian orientation to agriculture. He, along with John Jay, and James Madison, authored *The Federalist Papers*, a series of articles which were highly significant in the struggle to ratify the Constitution and which still are studied as outstanding statements of constitutional principles. In fact, Hamilton wrote a majority of the essays which comprise *The Federalist Papers*. Of him James Thomas Flexner wrote: "Hamilton did as much as any man—with the possible exception of Washington—to complete the Revolution by bringing the states together into a unified nation."[75]

---

* He may have been nineteen. Records differ as to whether he was born in 1755 or in 1757.

Hamilton served as secretary of the treasury during most of Washington's two terms, being, in effect, almost a prime minister. His leadership was vital in establishing for this country a sound fiscal and monetary basis. During his years of political ascendancy, there was little of spiritual significance recorded of him. The anti-Christian, violent nature of the French Revolution did shock him into the recognition that a Christian foundation is essential for there to be a successful society.

Hamilton lost to John Adams a power struggle for control of the Federalist Party. In retirement from office, his chance for the top gone, he changed for the better; his writings reflect a deepening Christian conviction. He, sadly, appears to have been one of those Christians who forgets the Lord when all is going well and who needs a dose of chastening as a corrective.

He now determined to establish the Christian Constitutional Society which would promote Christianity and the rule of law under the Constitution. It was to be organized with national leadership and state and local chapters. As part of its achieving its ends, the chapters would distribute literature and engage in charitable endeavors such as helping immigrants.[76] At the time of his death in 1804, however, it had not been developed.

John Jay: The Forgotten Founder

Regarding Aaron Burr as an unscrupulous man, not fit to hold office, Hamilton opposed him consistently and effectively, in particular thwarting Burr's attempts to become president and governor of New York. Burr challenged him to a duel. Hamilton's son Phillip had been killed in a duel and he strongly disapproved of the practice. He believed, though, that honor required him to accept the challenge, but resolved not to fire at Burr.

On the morning of July 11, 1804, they met. Hamilton was wounded fatally and died thirty-one hours later. During these hours, he testified to his faith in Christ as his Savior, forgave Burr, and requested and received Holy Communion from Benjamin Moore, the Episcopal Bishop of New York.

There was an intensive debate over slavery which threatened the fragile unity of the new country. The southern states, especially South Carolina and Georgia, had a high level of support for the institution and argued that it was essential to their economies. Of particular significance as leaders of this position at the Convention were four South Carolinians—Charles Cotesworth Pinckney, his younger second cousin Charles Pinckney, John Rutledge, and Pierce Butler. James Madison considered the most fundamental division of the states not to be on the basis of size, but on whether or not slavery was approved.

Prior to the Convention, Vermont and New Hampshire had prohibited slavery in their state constitutions, the Massachusetts Supreme Court had done so, Rhode Island and Pennsylvania had enacted laws ending it immediately, and Connecticut had passed a law calling for gradual emancipation, the approach which New York and New Jersey would take before long. At the Convention, delegates from New England and from most of the Middle Atlantic states called for terminating the slave trade at once, prohibiting slavery in the western territories, and adopting a plan for gradually freeing all slaves.[77]

A compromise avoided a split. The issue of slavery was not addressed directly in the Constitution. Article 1, section 9 permitted Congress to regulate or prohibit slave trading as of January 1, 1808.* Also, in calculating the population of states for the purpose of determining the number of seats in the House of Representatives, each slave would count as three-fifths of a free person.

Was the South bluffing? Would a constitutional prohibition of slavery or even of the slave trade have led to a walkout by several states? Benjamin Franklin feared so. For years he had been an opponent of slavery, although he owned house-

---

* At that time, it was banned.

John Jay: The Forgotten Founder

hold slaves. At the Convention, he talked of introducing a proposal condemning slavery, not just the slave trade. He was persuaded not to do so because of apprehension that the barely launched union could founder if the dispute were to surface.[78] Catherine Drinker Bowen wrote that "The Constitution could not have gone through without the slavery compromise."[79] She further said of those delegates who opposed slavery that "Without disrupting the Convention and destroying the Union they could do no more. The time was not yet come."[80]

What if there had been no compromise? What if North Carolina, South Carolina, and Georgia had seceded? Would the weakening effect of the division have made the two separate countries prey to European aggression? From the vantage point of historical perspective, one can conclude that this probably would not have happened. The British had little appetite for renewed conflict with North America, French internal problems were increasing, problems which would culminate in the Revolution of 1789, and Spain was continuing its gradual decline, a decline which would lead to the loss of most of its American territory in a few decades. Very likely, the two separate countries which would have emerged from a failed Philadelphia convention would some time later come back together. It is possible to wish for a stronger antislavery stance by the delegates in 1787, but, all things considered, the decision of the Convention was understandable given the years of struggle to form a country in the face of British opposition and all the internal bickering by men of little vision. Based on what was known by the men of 1787, their decision can be supported as wise.

The key thinkers among the founders, such as John Adams, Alexander Hamilton, and Jay, well understood the dangers of arbitrary government with a monarch having few checks on his power. They also, though, were equally aware of the destructive impact of unrestrained democracy or, as it also could be termed, democratic despotism. To some, this may sound like an oxymoron; after all, if there is democracy, how can there be despotism? Actually, reading the thoughts of Jean Jacques Rousseau, will make it quite simple. If the majority is unchecked by divine revelation or human constitution, it will become despotic:

> As nature gives each man absolute power over all his members, the social compact gives to the body politic absolute power over all its members also; and it is this power which, under the

direction of the general will, bears, as I have said, the name of Sovereignty.[81]

Rousseau, however, had no concerns that this would give rise to despotism. He averred that:

> Again, the Sovereign, being formed wholly of the individuals who compose it, neither has nor can have any interest contrary to theirs; and consequently the sovereign power need give no guarantee to its subjects, because it is impossible for the body to hurt all its members.[82]

The framers of the Constitution were determined to avoid both extremes. Expression would be given to the will of the majority, but there would be definite restraints on it. As was stated earlier, most of the fifty-five men in Philadelphia that summer were orthodox Christians. Even though they did not have the foresight, or depth, or strength to explicitly set forth such convictions in the document they wrote, they did believe that Christian influences would permeate the new country, holding in check the danger of democratic despotism. Further, while the House of Representatives would express directly the will of the electorate, the electoral college and the Senate would filter it and the Supreme Court would ensure that the Constitution was not violated. As John Adams trenchantly stated:

> The numbers of men in all ages have preferred ease, slumber, and good cheer to liberty.... We must not, then, depend alone upon the love of liberty in the soul of man for its preservation.... When the people who have no property feel the power in their own hands to determine all questions by a majority, they ever attack those who have property.... The multitude, therefore, as well as the nobles, must have a check.[83]

Sir Henry Sumner Maine, the brilliant nineteenth century British thinker, wrote of the danger to freedom and prosperity if the mass of the people were to discover that they can use the political process to gain economic advantages, to gain access to the wealth generated by others:

> ...if the mass of mankind were to make an attempt at redividing the common stock of good things, they

would resemble, not a number of claimants insisting on the fair division of a fund, but a mutinous crew, feasting on a ship's provisions, gorging themselves on the meat and intoxicating themselves with the liquors, but refusing to navigate the vessel to port.[84]

He further set forth his belief that:

You have only to tempt a portion of the population into temporary idleness by promising them a share in the fictitious hoard lying (as Mill puts it) in an imaginary strong-box which is supposed to contain all human wealth. You have only to take the heart out of those who would willingly labour and save, by taxing them *ad misericordiam* for the most laudable philanthropic objects. For it makes not the smallest difference to the motives of the thrifty and industrious part of mankind whether their fiscal oppressor be an Eastern despot, or a feudal baron, or a democratic legislature, and whether they are taxed for the benefit of a Corporation called Society, or for the advantage of an individual styled King or Lord.[85]

These points were understood well by most of the Founding Fathers, certainly by John Jay. They realized that a perfect government could not be established by human efforts. They were convinced, though, that their balancing of monarchical, aristocratic, and democratic influences would promote order, justice, and freedom for all. If, however, one of these elements were to push down the others, justice and freedom, possibly order too, would diminish. Also, the central government must be strong enough to protect a civilized society, but it must not be supreme; that is God's place.

On September 17, the Convention approved the new Constitution. Congress endorsed it on September 25 and sent it to the states for ratification. In the battle to come, Massachusetts, New York, Pennsylvania, and Virginia would be of primary significance. Those who favored ratification, the Federalists, were well-organized and well led by men such as John Jay, John Adams, Alexander Hamilton, and Benjamin Franklin. Their greatest advantage, though, was the widespread knowledge that George Washington supported the cause.

John Jay: The Forgotten Founder

They also profited from having lived under the weak, ineffectual government of the Articles of Confederation. Their opponents, the Antifederalists, also had outstanding men in their ranks, men such as Patrick Henry, Richard Henry Lee, Samuel Adams, George Mason, John Hancock, and Elbridge Gerry, who feared that the Constitution gave too much power to the national government. They lacked, however, George Washington and the organizational skills of the Federalists.

Over the two month period of December 1787-January 1788, five states ratified: Delaware (unanimously), Pennsylvania (46-23), New Jersey and Georgia (unanimously), and Connecticut (128-40). In February, Massachusetts ratified (187-168), the promise of a Bill of Rights swaying enough votes to overcome the opposition of Samuel Adams and John Hancock. That expectation also would help in other states. Maryland followed in April, approving the Constitution 63-11. South Carolina did so in May 149-73, New Hampshire in June 57-47 and Virginia the same month 89-79. Now, the requisite nine states had ratified the Constitution and it went into effect. In November 1789, North Carolina ratified 195-77 and in May 1790 Rhode Island did so 34-22.

Jay was elected to the New York state convention from solidly Federalist New York City.

Overall, though, the state was Antifederalist; of sixty-five delegates, only nineteen were Federalist. This disadvantage was overcome by several factors. First of all, the Federalist delegation included a number of outstanding leaders such as Jay, Alexander Hamilton, Chancellor Robert Livingston, Richard Morris, chief justice of the state Supreme Court, and James Duane, mayor of New York City. Furthermore, while the convention was meeting in Poughkeepsie, word arrived that New Hampshire and Virginia had ratified; nine states now had taken that step, meaning that the Constitution would go into effect. Finally, the Federalists used the carrot of supporting amendments desired by the Antifederalists, amendments which later became the Bill of Rights, and the stick of the possible secession of New York City from the rest of the state. Jay, who had good personal relations with people on both sides, was very effective behind the scenes, using the factors mentioned above plus his diplomatic skills, to gain the victorious margin.

Following through on the pledge to enact a Bill of Rights, on March 4, 1789 Congress proposed and submitted to the states twelve amendments. Two of them, one dealing with congressional representation, the other with congressional pay, were rejected. The other ten were ratified effective December 15, 1791.

John Jay: The Forgotten Founder

The delegates produced a document which has passed the test of time, being the oldest written constitution still in effect. Learning from their experiences with the highly centralized British government, they, through debate and compromise, created a balance of power between the national government and the states and between the executive, legislative, and judicial branches which were separate but interrelated. Also learning from their experiences with the Articles of Confederation, they established a government with the requisite powers to be effective and respected through, for example, having the power to tax and to control interstate commerce.

If all people were virtuous, any system of government would work and if all were corrupt, justice and freedom could not survive; order could exist only if they were extinguished. The best that human beings can do is to devise a political structure which will maximize the prospects for order, justice, and freedom while minimizing the potentiality for the breakdown of them.

The United States Constitution has stood through the years, serving as a model for many throughout the world. It hits an excellent balance, being amendable to reflect changing conditions, but only if the determination to do so is great and is maintained for a long period of time. The character of the American people has been a key factor in making it work and last.

The Federalist Papers

The Federalist Papers generally is regarded as the most significant work in the history of U.S. political thought and as one of the classics of Western Civilization. Representing the efforts of Alexander Hamilton, James Madison, and John Jay, three first-rate thinkers who also were men of impressive achievement, it played a key role in the campaign to ratify the Constitution.

Jay's poor health during the autumn of 1787 precluded his writing more than five of *The Federalist Papers*, as against 26 by Madison, 51 by Hamilton, and three jointly by Madison and Hamilton, yet his thought was significant and influential. In these writings, he expressed with clarity his views as a strong central government conservative, convinced that a confederation (a voluntary association of quasi-independent states) would promote disunity and weakness. In number 2 he opposed the idea that "instead of looking for safety and happiness in union, we ought to seek it in a division of the States into distinct confederacies or sovereignties."[86] He emphasized that this country had been blessed by Providence with geographical unity, good soil, plus oceans and rivers for communication.

Also in the same number 2, Jay rather overstated the extent to which the American people were united:

> With equal pleasure I have as often taken notice that Providence has been pleased to give this one connected country to one united people—a people descended from the same ancestors, speaking the same language, professing the same religion, attached to the same principles of government, very similar in their manners and customs, and who, by their joint counsels, arms, and efforts, fighting side by side throughout a long and bloody war, have nobly established their general liberty and independence.[87]

Although the United States in the 1780s was less diverse than the country today, there was a significant amount of variety back then. In 1774, the total population of the British colonies which became the United States was less than 3,000,000.*

---

* The first formal national census was in 1790.

Of this figure, 200,000 to 250,000 were of German origin. About 60,000 people were of Dutch descent. A further 35,000 were French Huguenot in background.[88] Jay himself was of this ancestry. These groups maintained pride in their heritage and passed this on to their descendents.

Yet, there is definite fundamental truth in Jay's assertion since these people did assimilate into a political and judicial system British in origin. Furthermore, this became an English-speaking country. Also, although there was denominational variety, the country overwhelmingly was Christian. In addition, there is forged a powerful bond between those who have fought alongside each other in a common cause. So, Jay's assertion can be regarded as somewhat overstated, but in general it accurately depicts this country at the dawn of independence.

It was his conviction that the national government would attract the most outstanding people, out-competing the states so that, as he set forth in number 3, "the national government will be more wise, systematical, and judicious," than state governments.[89] He then affirmed that:

> Hence, it will result that the administration, the political counsels, and the judicial decisions of the national gov-

ernment will be more wise, systematical, and judicious than those of individual States, and consequently more satisfactory with respect to other nations, as well as more safe with respect to us.[90]

In the same paper, Jay stated his conviction that national defense is the first priority of the United States government and that a country united under a strong central government will best preserve security against enemies foreign and domestic. Furthermore, wars would be less likely under this type of government than under a confederation of sovereign states in that there would be fewer aggravations with one government handling security and a more deliberate, cool response to those which did occur.[91]

He continued in number 4 to elucidate his conviction that the national government would attract the most talented individuals from all parts of the country, rising above regional interests and focusing on policies which are best for all. This would be of particular significance in reference to national defense. A strong union will discourage aggression whereas an America divided into several independent entities would be weaker in terms of armies and fleets. He further developed this theme in number 5. Disunity invites danger from foreign foes, a point he demonstrated drawing upon European history. Here, Jay was reacting to the all too frequent disunity during the War for Independence when states often were reluctant to send their armed forces far from their borders, not seeing well enough the whole picture, the need for unified vision and action.

In number 64, Jay addressed the procedure for making treaties from the vantage point of the American most experienced in diplomacy, the leading or a leading figure in several of the most important treaties into which this country entered during its early years. He opened with praise for the indirect procedures by which the president and members of the United States Senate were chosen, the former by electors selected by the voters in each state, the latter by state legislatures elected by these voters. He believed this would mean that these choices would be in the hands of

> . . . those men only who have become the most distinguished by their abilities and virtue, and in whom the people perceive just grounds for confidence.[92]

He further averred that a body such as the House of Representatives, "a popular assembly composed of members constantly coming and going in quick succession,"[93] would not be capable of dealing with great matters which require not just substantial talent, but also knowledge and the time to study and evaluate these matters.*

Jay set forth strongly his view that treaties must be accepted as the supreme law of the land, as stipulated in Article VI of the Constitution, or this country would find it difficult to enter into agreements with others. Even though treaties, as is true of laws, may be altered or repealed, they must be considered binding unless repealed.

Although Jay's contributions were limited because of health considerations, once more he demonstrated the scholarship, sound thinking, and clarity of expression for which he was held in high regard.

---

* Jay also took into account the two year terms for House members as against the six year terms for senators, assuming frequent turnover in the membership of the House. Today, for a variety of reasons, there is limited turnover.

Chief Justice

Washington was sworn in as the first president of the United States on April 30, 1789 at Federal Hall in New York, having been chosen unanimously by the electoral college; no other chief executive has been so honored. He offered Jay a choice of positions.* His preference was to be the first chief justice of the Supreme Court. Of him Bruce Chadwick stated that:

> Jay certainly had the proper judicial and administrative credentials to serve as the head of the court, but it was his friendship with Washington, formed during dozens of dinners in

---

* Willard Sterne Randall maintained that Jay did not get to be secretary of state because Washington was concerned about resentment of Jay by westerners because he had been willing to yield temporarily American claims to free navigation of the Mississippi River in negotiations with Spain in return for their giving us trading rights with their New World colonies. Washington accepted Madison's advice that selecting Jefferson as secretary of state would allay western opposition and bind the country together. (Willard Sterne Randall, *George Washington: A Life* [New York: Henry Holt and Company, 1997], 458).

winter camp at Morristown, that earned him the job.[94]

Initially, the Court consisted of the chief justice and five associate justices. Serving with Jay were five men with distinguished records in the law and in politics: James Wilson of Pennsylvania; John Rutledge of South Carolina; William Cushing of Massachusetts; John Blair of Virginia; and James Iredell of North Carolina.

As the first person to hold this position, Jay established a number of precedents, among them his ceasing to wear the traditional judicial wig. More significant was his assertion in the case of Glass v. Sloop Betsy that the federal courts had jurisdiction over the activities of foreign governments on U.S. soil. The new French revolutionary government was at war with Britain, a conflict in which the Washington Administration was determined to maintain neutrality. The Federalists, although firm supporters of independence, were closer to English political and judicial principles, while the Antifederalists were more enamored of the new France. The Betsy, owned by Swedish and American interests, was captured by a French privateer and taken as a prize into Baltimore where the French consul assumed jurisdiction over her. The Swedish owners sued in federal District Court to regain her, arguing that the French Consul had no power of adjudication. The American government opposed having French privateers seize ships and bring them into American ports where French prize courts could sell them. Prohibiting this, however, required the support of federal courts. The government lost at the District Court and Circuit Court levels where rulings were handed down that our courts did not have jurisdiction.

The case was appealed to the Supreme Court which heard it in February 1794. The Court ruled unanimously that federal courts can determine the legality of prizes taken into American ports, that no other country can establish any type of court in the United States except through treaty, and that the admiralty jurisdiction of the French Consul was not valid.[95] American neutrality was upheld.

Another important ruling of the Jay Court was Chisholm v. Georgia. Prior to the outbreak of the war for independence, a Georgia man moved to Britain after accepting the bonds of his two partners to settle the business arrangement. After he died, his executors, two South Carolinians, tried to collect the bonds, but the two former partners had opposed American independence and their property had been confiscated by Georgia. The executors sued to collect from Georgia whose attorneys argued that the Supreme Court had no jurisdiction.

This contention was rejected, the Court ruling that citizens of one state could bring an original suit before them against another state for breach of contract. Article III of the Constitution stipulated that United States courts had jurisdiction over disputes between a state and citizens of another state. By inference, a state could be sued as well as bring suits.

Jay tended to see the states as administrative districts with a relationship to the national government corresponding to that of counties to the states of which they are a part. The next year, 1794, Congress formally proposed the XI Amendment to the Constitution and submitted it to the states. On January 5, 1798, announcement was made of its ratification. It said that:

> The Judicial power of the United States shall not be construed to extend to any suit in law or equity, commenced or prosecuted against one of the United States by Citizens of another State, or by Citizens or subjects of any Foreign State.

Now the federal courts no longer would have jurisdiction in such cases. No state could be sued by citizens of another state.

John Jay: The Forgotten Founder

At this time in our history, the Supreme Court consisted of the chief justice and five associate justices. Thirteen federal district courts had their own judges. In between these two levels were three circuit courts, each of which had two Supreme Court justices and one district court judge assigned to it. The Supreme Court justices rode these circuits meeting with the district court judges. This created difficult situations in which a Supreme Court justice who originally made a ruling would hear the appeal of it. Furthermore, Jay did not enjoy the grind of circuit riding, nor did he consider this frequent moving about the best way for these men to grow in the law as well as if they were able to remain in one place and deal with the cases brought before them.

In 1792, supporters of Jay's entered his name in the New York gubernatorial election, challenging incumbent George Clinton. Slavery became an issue in the campaign, Jay's opponents using his antislavery convictions to rally opposition to him. Although not campaigning actively, Jay did respond on slavery, stating that:

> In my opinion every man, of every colour and description, has a natural right to freedom, and I shall ever acknowledge myself to be an advocate

for the manumission of slaves, in such way as may be consistent with the justice due to them with the justice due to their masters, and with the regard due to the actual state of society. These considerations unite in convincing me that the abolition of slavery must necessarily be gradual.[96]

He further set forth his belief that:

To promote, by virtuous means, the extension of the blessings of liberty, to protect a poor and friendless race of men, their wives, and children, from the snares and violence of men-stealers, to provide instruction for children who were destitute of the means of education, and who, instead of pernicious, will now become useful members of society, are certainly objects and cares of which no man has reason to be ashamed, and for which no man ought to be censured.[97]

Jay lost a close election because of legal technicalities, concerning how the ballots from two counties were handled. County sheriffs were required by law to forward ballots to the secretary of state where then they were to be turned over to a committee of canvassers appointed by the state legislature. A majority of them were Clinton supporters. The determination of which man would win came down to the votes of Otsego and Tioga Counties. The Jay totals in the two counties were large enough to give him the governorship. Both sets of ballots, though, were excluded by the canvassers. The Otsego County ballots had been forwarded by a sheriff whose commission had expired and those of Tioga County by a deputy sheriff who had not been given a written authorization. As a result of this throwing out of the ballots, Clinton was returned to office by 108 votes.[98]

Jay's antislavery convictions remained unshaken. When he later was elected governor of New York, he took the lead in providing for the emancipation of slaves in the state.

During the four years he served as chief justice, Jay's integrity, dedication to the Constitution, knowledge of the law, and ability established confidence in the new court and in the other federal courts. His insistence on the independence of the judiciary did much to solidify the separation of powers. For example, he rejected Hamilton's call that he join in attacking the Virginia resolutions opposing the assumption of state debts by the national government. As a Federalist, it was not so much that Jay disagreed with Hamilton as that he believed that the Supreme Court should not be involved in politics. When Washington once requested the advice of the Supreme Court, Jay responded that it was not right for the court to give opinions on cases not formally before it.

Walter Stahr credited Jay with impressive accomplishments during his years as the first chief justice, stating of him that:

> He did not make the Supreme Court the power it would be under John Marshall, but he helped define what federal courts could do, such as review statutes for constitutionality, and what they could not do, such as decide abstract questions.[99]

Although the courts of this country are by no means uninvolved in politics, Jay's actions did further the principle of judicial independence.

Jay's Treaty

While still serving as chief justice, Jay was selected by President Washington to serve as head of the American delegation to negotiate a treaty with Britain dealing with a number of contentious issues. For one thing, the British had not yet withdrawn from the military positions they still occupied in the Northwest Territory, posts they had agreed to leave in the 1783 Treaty of Paris. Among them were such strategic locations as Detroit, Michilimackinac, Oswego, and Niagara. They and other posts controlled the Great Lakes and the Lake Champlain-Hudson River invasion route. The British argued that the Americans had not yet satisfied debts owed British creditors, thereby justifying their remaining. In addition, the British were aiding Indians in order to prevent more American expansion in the region. Complicating matters further, there were trade disputes, questions concerning navigation rights on the Mississippi River, and British interference with shipping. After extensive talks, the treaty was signed in London on November 19, 1794. It actually was beneficial to both sides.

The Life of John Jay

Back in the United States Jay was castigated, unfairly, by the Jeffersonian Democratic-Republicans* for betraying American interests to the British. The treaty did not deal with the impressments of sailors serving on American ships, it did not secure British adherence to international maritime law; American trade with France, with whom the British were at war, still would be stopped by the seizure of American ships. Also, the British had not paid American slave owners for the slaves who left with them at the end of the war.

The British, though, did agree to evacuate their posts. Jay refused to yield on American navigation of the Mississippi and rejected the British hope to bring further south the border with Canada. We agreed to pay prewar debts owed to British subjects, ultimately £600,000. The British in turn paid £1,317,000 for American vessels taken wrongfully. They would continue to put tariffs on American products while the United States granted most-favored nation trade status to Britain. In turn, American and British ships would have equal privileges in Britain and in the East Indies. American trade with the British West Indies would be limited

---

* By the end of Washington's first term, the Antifederalists had adopted the more positive designation Democratic-Republicans. By the time of the Jackson Administration, they would be simply Democrats.

to ships no larger than seventy tons. Since ships of this size could not cross the Atlantic safely, this meant that these ships had to go to American ports where their cargoes had to be transferred to larger vessels, adding time and cost to the transactions.

From the beginning, Jay was playing a weak hand. After independence had been secured, the United States had demobilized most of the army and navy, our capabilities now being insignificant in comparison with those of the British. Of course, the British did have their hands full confronting the new revolutionary government of France and had no desire to renew the conflict with the Americans. In a letter to Washington written from London on June 23, 1794, Jay observed that "The war with France is popular, and that a war with us would be unpopular."[100] This estimate of the situation was accurate, indicating that Jay had lost none of his diplomatic analytical skills. Still, since we were not prepared for war with Britain, Jay could not push too far lest the British decide to rethink their reluctance to fight us.

Also exacerbating Jay's problems was the advance intelligence the British had concerning the American stance going into the talks. Alexander Hamilton, preferring Britain to the new radical government of France which he considered a danger to civilized order, had told George Hammond, the British minister (ambassador) to the United States that we would not insist on neutral rights vis-à-vis the British blockade of France. We would not object to the British argument that foodstuffs were contraband and could be confiscated from neutral ships. Furthermore, we would not maintain the claim that French goods being carried on American ships should be free from seizure by the British.[101]

While in England negotiating the treaty, Jay became friendly with William Wilberforce, an influential member of the House of Commons, a fellow Christian of the Anglican persuasion, and a fellow abolitionist. They discussed in person and began a correspondence on how to bring about, initially, the stopping of the slave trade and later ending slavery altogether. The correspondence continued for years, the friendship and mutual respect transcending the growing problems between their homelands which arose during the opening decade and a half of the nineteenth century. The depth of their Christianity and their determined opposition to slavery were bonds of great strength.[102]

When news of the treaty arrived in this country, reaction was heated, largely from those who opposed the Washington Administration. Now that we were independent, the Federalists regarded the British as preferable to the French, especially the revolutionary government which they considered a threat to freedom and peace. The Democratic-Republicans regarded the French Revolution as being akin to ours, as the harbinger of a new era of freedom for France. A treaty, therefore, which benefited Britain was anathema to them. Washington supported the treaty as a solid achievement under the circumstances, although, as he stated in a letter to Gouverneur Morris on December 22, 1795, "one could have wished for more favorable terms."[103] His confidence in Jay never wavered. On June 26, 1796, he wrote to Alexander Hamilton that he had "great confidence in the abilities, and purity of Mr. Jay's views, as well as his experience."[104] In the Senate, the vote to ratify the treaty was strictly along party lines, just meeting the constitutionally mandated two thirds margin.

From the vantage point of historical perspective, Jay's Treaty today is considered the best that could have been achieved under the circumstances. Joseph Ellis, for example, was convinced that Jay did well, that the historical consensus is that the treaty favored the British, but that it was a "shrewd bargain" for the United States since the British now would withdraw their soldiers, opening up the West to American development, and American trade would benefit greatly.[105] Also concurring was Walter McDougall who labeled Jay's Treaty a success for this country, especially when taking into account British power.[106] Thomas Fleming too supported Jay's diplomatic efforts as bringing positive gains for this country.[107] David McCullough agreed, referring to the position of John Adams that, considering the odds against Jay, the treaty was the right thing to do, being far better than a war with Britain at that time.[108] Ron Chernow wrote that Jay had ensured peace with Britain at a time when the United States was ill-prepared for war and gained access for this country to lucrative overseas markets.[109]

John Lamberton Harper believed that Hamilton probably would have gotten along better with Grenville than did Jay, but does not believe that he would have pushed harder in the negotiations and that overall the treaty concluded would not have been substantially different.[110] Theodore Roosevelt's position was similar; he suggested that: "Perhaps a man like Hamilton might have procured rather better terms; but, taken as a whole, it worked an immense improvement upon the condition of things already existing."[111]

John Ferling, though, disagreed, alleging that "Evidence exists that Britain would have relinquished more had Jay pushed harder."[112] Samuel Flagg Bemis agreed, stating that Jay was weak, controlled by Hamilton, outmaneuvered by Grenville, and that the treaty was a mistake for the United States.[113] Joining with them was Richard Norton Smith who argued that Jay, "instructed to secure American rights and open British markets,"[114] had not succeeded in accomplishing either. In addition, Winston Churchill joined the critics, making reference to "Jay's ineptitude in negotiation."[115] To the contrary, it is not likely that Jay could have gained more given the realities of the time. Of course, as fascinating as counter-factual history is, there is no way to prove what might have been.

There were political consequences for Jay. Hamilton, recognizing that his prospects for becoming the second president of the United States were not good, commented that the most likely successors to Washington were John Adams, Thomas Jefferson, and John Jay.[116] The attacks on Jay, however, were so vehement that his stock nationally fell and the mantle of Washington fell on Adams. Washington, however, continued to have confidence in him as did most Federalists, especially those in New York. Also, chambers of commerce in Boston, New York, Philadelphia, and Charleston supported the treaty as being good for American economic interests.

The attacks on Jay were extensive and vitriolic. James Thomson Callender wrote of "Jay's desertion" of American interests and of "Jay's capitulation" to British interests.[117] A mob in Philadelphia carried an effigy of him in a parade. The effigy had a pair of scales, one designated "American Liberty and Independence," and the other "British Gold." From the mouth of the figure came the words, "Come up to my price, and I will sell you my Country." The effigy then was burned.[118] Reportedly Jay gave vent to his wry sense of humor commenting that he could go from one end of the country to the other by the light of burning effigies.[119]

The print media were highly partisan. Some of the Federalist journals wished fewer concessions had been made by Jay, but most, such as John Fenno's *Gazette of the United States*, supported him. The opposition press, in particular Benjamin Franklin Baches's[*] *Aurora* castigated him for abandoning what was best for this country and selling out to the British.

Eric Burns has contended that the fight over the treaty was so long and so bitter that it made permanent the two-party system in this country.[120] Perhaps so; certainly this was an extended and rancorous clash, but such a division was almost inevitable, this being a free country with human beings inhabiting it. Actually, opposition to the

---

[*] He was the grandson of Benjamin Franklin.

John Jay: The Forgotten Founder

Washington Administration already had developed, coalescing around Thomas Jefferson who had resigned as secretary of state the previous year.

It is interesting to note that, although he never was a candidate for president or vice president, Jay did receive electoral college votes in 1789, 1796, and 1800. At that time, each elector cast two votes. The person who came in first was elected president, the second place finisher became vice president, assuming each had a majority. In 1789, every elector cast a vote for Washington, a total of sixty-nine. John Adams was second with thirty-four, Jay third with nine. The remaining twenty-six electoral votes were scattered among nine other men. There were some Federalists outside of New England who did not want Adams to serve as vice president. In 1796, when Adams was elected, Jay received five votes, finishing behind seven other contenders. One elector cast a ballot for Jay in 1800, the year Jefferson won a bitterly contested race. In both of these elections, Jay supported Adams for president and sought no votes for himself.

The Life of John Jay

Governor of New York

In spite of the political attacks on him because of the treaty, Jay's support base in New York remained firm. As was discussed earlier, he barely lost the 1792 gubernatorial election to George Clinton because of questionable technicalities. In 1795, while still in London, he again was nominated by the Federalists and this time was elected by a solid majority. During this period, the term of office was three years. In neither 1792 nor 1795 did Jay campaign actively, but simply let his record, his abilities, and his character speak for themselves. On June 25, he resigned as chief justice and was inaugurated governor on July 1. By this time, he was not reluctant to leave the Supreme Court, primarily because of the burden of traveling the circuits, as the justices then were required to do. Also, he was very much in disagreement with the opposition by Congress to establishing circuit courts with their own judges, sparing Supreme Court justices the burden of frequent travel.

When Jay became governor, the practice of declaring a day of thanksgiving to God, standard in New England, had not been instituted in New York. In November 1795, after the passing of a severe yellow fever assault, he issued a proclamation of thanksgiving to God.

As governor, Jay continued his opposition to slavery, now being in a position to do something concrete. He took the lead in getting enacted in April 1799 a bill to end it in New York. Earlier proposals to do so had foundered on the question of compensating slave owners. The Jay plan avoided that reef by providing for gradual emancipation. The bill stipulated that all children born to slaves after July 4 of that year would be free with the proviso that females serve apprenticeships until they were twenty-five, males until age twenty-eight. This was to ensure that they were prepared to take their places in society as free individuals. Also, the bill prohibited exporting slaves. The gradual emancipation approach avoided conflict over compensation and allayed the fears of those who feared the social impact of suddenly freeing people unprepared for the responsibilities of freedom.[121]

He also advocated decent treatment of Indians, but believed that their becoming civilized could take generations. He saw several key problems which needed to be overcome:

> Is there not reason to apprehend that, until the savages can be prevailed upon to dwell in fixed habitations, to

have separate property, and to depend more on husbandry than the chase for subsistence, little success will attend the best efforts to civilize or christianize [lower case c in letter] them?[122]

Later Jay added the observation that "Indian men regard labor as degrading, and fit only for women and slaves. Prejudices associated with a sense of honor are not easily overcome."[123]

Although a supporter of the death penalty in principle, Jay believed that execution was the punishment for too many crimes; at the time, for example, burglary and forgery were hanging offenses. He succeeded in persuading the legislature to reduce the application of capital punishment to treason, murder, assisting in murder, and theft from churches. Until the new law went into effect, Jay stayed the execution of those convicted of capital offenses other than the four above ones. Normally, though, he was chary in granting pardons or otherwise interfering in the criminal justice system.

During the last months of Jay's second (and last) term as governor, the Democratic-Republicans won control of the legislature and chose a new Council of Appointments which refused to approve Jay's nominations, the three Democratic-Republicans and one Federalist voting along party lines. In one case, to fill a vacancy in the position of sheriff of Dutchese County, the Council rejected eight consecutive nominations by Jay. Finally, he nominated a fellow party member of the Council majority who then was confirmed. In general, though, Jay stood his ground, a number of significant positions remaining vacant until George Clinton again was elected in April 1801, Jay having decided to retire.[124]

But, before he left public office, a more significant crisis, one with national implications, would arise and confront Jay with a clear choice between principle and party loyalty. By 1800, he had determined to retire from elective politics, tired from years of active toil in both national and state government, serving in the executive, legislative, and judicial branches. In addition, although he would live to be eighty-three, dying in 1829, his health was not consistently robust and that of his wife was beginning to fail. Also, in 1800, the Jeffersonians for the first time gained control of both houses of Congress. Twice during the previous six Congresses they had controlled the House of Representatives (1791-1793 and 1793-1795), but previously never had the Senate. New York was one of the states which they had won from the Federalists. With control of the legislature in their hands, they would choose the twelve electors from the state, swinging it out of the Adams column where it had been in 1796 into that of Jefferson.

Alexander Hamilton now showed a darker side of the brilliance which he had used to such great effect in establishing this country on a solid economic footing. His innovative skill was to be clearly evident but his ethical compass he ignored in his determination to block the election of Jefferson. Hamilton was by no means a fervent supporter of John Adams, but he was a true Federalist who regarded Jefferson's commitment to the Constitution rather shaky, that a Jefferson Administration would bring back an extreme states' rights position such as that which plagued the country during the days when we were governed by the Articles of Confederation. Hamilton proposed that Jay convene a special session of the lame duck Federalist legislature and change the selection of presidential electors by the legislature to a popular vote by districts. The Federalists might have been able to control enough district elections to reelect Adams. Hamilton lobbied hard for this scheme, recognizing that there were problems with it, but regarding the bad consequences of a Jefferson presidency as outweighing any objections to his proposal. Furthermore, Philip Schuyler, one of the more prominent citizens of the state and a former general, also urged adoption of the idea.[125]

Jay shared Hamilton's concerns about Jefferson, but his Christian convictions, respect for proper procedure, and for the will of the voters were too strong for him to engage in such shenanigans. He took no action, the scheme died, and Jefferson became the third president of the United States.[126]

Although Adams had lost his bid for reelection, he would continue to be president until March 1801.* In the middle of December, Oliver Ellsworth submitted his resignation as chief justice. Adams did not want to leave the country without a chief justice until March, but also, he certainly did not want to give Jefferson the opportunity to fill a position of such significance. Feeling estranged from his fellow Federalists, he did not discuss replacement ideas with senators of his party then in Washington for a lame-duck congressional session. On December 19, he wrote Jay, asking him to return as chief justice. This was the best choice Adams could have made. In spite of the controversy concerning the treaty with the British, Jay was widely respected, was a staunch Federalist who

---

* In 1933, the Twentieth Amendment changed the date of presidential inaugurations to the January 20 following the election.

was independent of Hamilton's domination (although acceptable to Hamilton and his followers), and was certain to be confirmed by the Senate.

Adams earnestly urged Jay to heed the call to serve his country again, stating that:

> The firmest security we can have against the effects of visionary schemes or fluctuating theories, will be in a solid judiciary; and nothing will cheer the hopes of the best men so much as your acceptance of this appointment....[127]

He went on to express his pessimism at the direction in which the country was moving as a result of the election, that Jay's acceptance would be a means "of furnishing my country with the best security its inhabitants afforded against the increaseing dissolution of morals."[128]*

Adams, though, was prepared for Jay's likely refusal to return to the Court. His alternative

---

* Adams and Jefferson had been friends and colleagues in the movement for independence, but now they had separated in both categories because of the Federalist/Democratic-Republican philosophical and policy differences. After both were in retirement, the friendship and mutual respect were revived, although the philosophical differences remained.

plan would be to promote Justice William Paterson to be chief justice and Jared Ingersoll, United States district attorney in Philadelphia, would be appointed to fill the vacancy created by Ellsworth's resignation.

On January 2, Jay responded, expressing his appreciation of the honor, but declining, reiterating his opposition to the burdensome system of circuit riding to which he had objected when he resigned as chief justice. He further affirmed that his health was not sufficiently robust to serve again.[129] Retirement with Sarah now appealed far more than a return to the arena.

At this stage, Adams stepped back from his aforementioned second choice. The lame-duck Federalist Congress had passed a judicial reform bill creating six federal circuit courts with three judges each, sparing the Supreme Court justices that duty and permitting them to remain in Washington. Had he known of this, Jay might have decided differently, but probably not since he was ready to retire from public life. Also, the Supreme Court was reduced from six justices to five.* As the end of his term in office drew near, Adams now believed that it would be better to select as chief justice someone not presently on the Court who could be confirmed

---

* The present size of nine was adopted in 1869.

readily and not attempt to get a sixth justice on the bench just prior to when the new law would go into effect. Were he to do the latter, when a vacancy occurred, the new president would not be able to choose a successor since the Court then would be down to the new level of five justices. Although he certainly wanted to limit Jefferson's opportunities to control the Supreme Court as well as the executive and legislative branches, still choosing a sixth justice was too offensive to the Adams sense of propriety.

At this time, he turned to Secretary of State John Marshall who was confirmed by the lame-duck Senate and served as chief justice until his death in 1835, the last Federalist to hold high office. It is interesting to note that this man, generally considered the greatest chief justice in our history, was greeted with little enthusiasm by the Federalists in the Senate who regarded him as too independent of party control. They delayed confirmation until January 27 when, convinced that Adams would not give them a better choice, they accepted him.

The Life of John Jay

The Bedford Years

In May 1801, Jay ended his twenty-seven years of public service and moved to his retirement home in Bedford, about thirty miles north of New York City. The property had been acquired by his grandfather, Jacobus van Cortland, around 1700. Jay had inherited it from his father and until now had leased it to a tenant. Now he undertook to expand the existing home into something more befitting a gentleman of his status. Through the summer and autumn he directed the work of renovation in the company of his teenage daughter Ann. Sarah, suffering declining health, stayed with her sister during the remodeling. Of the children other than Ann, Peter was engaged in the practice of law with his cousin, Peter Munro. Maria was married to Goldsborough Bayner Jr., scion of a politically and economically prominent family, and was living in Albany. Living with her and her husband were twelve-year-old William and Sarah Louisa, two years younger.

Jay's love of his family, of the property, and general sentimentality were demonstrated in a letter he wrote to his son, Peter, in 1792, reflecting on his father's having planted many trees and that "I never walk in their shade without deriving additional pleasure from that circumstance; the time will come when you will probably experience similar emotions."[130]

Financially Jay would live a comfortable retirement thanks to his having invested in New York City real estate which both appreciated in value and produced income. In addition, there was income from the Bedford farming operation.

In December, Sarah rejoined her husband in their new home. It was a three story house with a porch across the front, a sloping lawn, and views of the countryside with hills in the distance.* Their time together there, though, was to be short; she died in May. It was then that Jay led the grieving children from the deathbed into the next room where he read to them 1 Corinthians 15, reminding them of the promise of eternal life with Christ for those who are His. Jay's faith sustained him and comforted him, but in this world, the void created by Sarah's death never was filled during the twenty-seven years remaining until his death in May 1829. Ann stayed with him through these years. William would be with him until he left for

---

*Today the Jay homestead is owned by the state of New York and administered by the Office of Parks, Recreation and Historic Preservation as a state historic site. It has been restored to appear as it did during the years of Jay's occupancy.

John Jay: The Forgotten Founder

Yale in 1804. He returned to Bedford upon graduation, married, involved himself with the farm, and became prominent as a founder of the American Bible Society,* as a judge and as a leader in the abolition movement. Sarah Louisa visited frequently with her father, although she generally was with Maria in Albany.

In his rather quiet retirement, Jay continued his efforts for the gradual end of slavery and the successful integration of the former slaves into American society. As part of this endeavor, he was a leader in establishing the New York School for Free Africans to further their transition from bondage to freedom.

He also was active in running his estate, concerning himself with the crops and animals. Furthermore, he studied better ways to farm, such as improved fertilizer.

He still followed issues of public policy, although he no longer was involved actively in the political wars. His interest, though, continued. In 1821, Jay expressed his convictions on taxation in a

---

*Its founding in 1816 led to a serious dispute between William Jay and Episcopal Bishop John Henry Hobart, a high churchman who opposed interdenominational Bible societies. While supporting Bible reading and personal devotion, Hobart emphasized the necessity for Christian work to be carried on through the organized church. The two of them engaged in a prolonged written and verbal debate.

letter to Governor Brown of Ohio. He stated that although governments do have constitutional authority to tax, they must be careful not to make difficult productive activity. He, therefore, questioned the wisdom of "taxing the products of beneficial labor, either mental or manual...."[131] He preferred not to tax either property or income, but did set forth some considerations if property were to be taxed:

> Whether taxation should extend only to property, or only to income, or to both, are points on which opinions have not been uniform. I am inclined to think, that both should not be taxed. If the first is preferred, then tax the land and stock of a farmer, but not his crops; tax his milk-cows, but not their milk, nor the butter and cheese made of it, whether the same be sent to market or consumed in his family. Tax the real and personal estate of a physician and a lawyer, but not the conjectural and varying profits they derive from the skillful and Industrious exercise of their professsions, etc., etc.[132]

Jay's public policy views were consistent. He believed that government, especially the national government, must have clear-cut powers, but that these powers must be limited in scope. Care must be exercised so that productive economic enterprise would not be hampered by bad tax policy.

He believed firmly in freedom and in representative government, but not in universal suffrage; he advocated limiting the franchise to the productive, to the achievers. In a letter to William Wilberforce written on October 25, 1810, Jay stated that:

> It is not a new remark, that they who own the country are the most fit persons to participate in the government of it. This remark, with certain restrictions and exceptions, has force in it; and applies both to the elected and the electors, though with most force to the former.[133]

Hereditary factors would not control who voted and who held office; people in freedom could rise and fall as their talents and perseverance determined. Here Jay, born into the upper socio/economic level was in full accord with the modestly born Alexander Hamilton and John Adams who rose on ability and drive.

In terms of national security, his common sense again was evident. In a November 13, 1790 letter to Washington, Jay set forth his conviction that "Peace is the time to prepare for defense against hostilities."[134] All too often throughout our history, this prudent advice has been ignored by our fellow citizens.

During the years at Bedford, Jay's health had its ups and downs. He enjoyed early morning horseback riding and did involve himself in overseeing the work of the farm. Overall, though, his health was not robust and the 1820s saw his physical condition decline; he suffered a mild stroke in 1825 from which he did recover. By the spring of 1829, it was clear that the end was near. At eighty-three, Jay was ready to leave this world to enter eternal life with his Lord and to be again with Sarah. On May 27, he died peacefully and his body was interred in the family cemetery at nearby Rye.

The Bedford estate was inherited by William Jay. He and his brother Peter jointly inherited their father's manuscript books and correspondence. They carefully controlled access to the material. For example, Jared Sparks, the historian and president of Harvard who had criticized Jay, was prevented from using the material. William spent four years editing everything and, with commentary added, published *The Life of John Jay* in 1833. Although it is a useful reference work, Jay's work is too much a panegyric, something unnecessary since John Jay can stand on his own as a figure of great significance. The over-protectiveness of William Jay was a mistake.[135]

End Notes

[1] 1 Peter 1:24-25.

[2] Hamilton, Madison, and Jay, *The Federalist Papers* (New York: Mentor, 1961), 31-37.

[3] Walter Stahr, *John Jay: Founding Father* (New York: Hambledon and London, 2005), 3.

[4] William Wilson Manross, *A History of the American Episcopal Church* (New York: Morehouse Publishing Co., 1935), 114, 178.

[5] John Eidsmoe, *Christianity and the Constitution: The Faith of our Founding Fathers* (Grand Rapids, Michigan: Baker Books, 1987), 165.

[6] Manross, *A History of the American Episcopal Church,* 123-124.

[7] Richard Morris, ed., *John Jay: The Making of a Revolutionary* [Unpublished Papers 1745-1780] (New York: Harper and Row, Publishers, 1975), 55.

[8] Susan Mary Alsop, *Yankees at the Court: The First Americans in Paris* (Garden City, New York: Doubleday and Company, Inc., 1982), 45, 219; David McCullough, *John Adams* (New York: Simon and Schuster, 2001), 300.

[9] J. F. C. Fuller, *A Military History of the Western World, Vol. II: From the Defeat of the Spanish Armada, 1588, to the Battle of Waterloo, 1815* (New York: Funk and Wagnalls Company, 1955), 270.

[10] Edmund S. Morgan, *Benjamin Franklin* (New Haven, Connecticut: Yale University Press, 2002), 83-84, 89.

[11] Edmund Burke, *Selected Writings and Speeches*, ed. by Peter J. Stanlis (Chicago: Regnery Gateway, 1963), 149.

End Notes: The Life of John Jay

¹² John Jay, *The Correspondence and Public Papers of John Jay*, ed. by Henry P. Johnston (4 vols.; New York: Burt Franklin, 1890-93), IV, 270-273. Hereinafter referred to as Jay, *Correspondence and Public Papers*.

¹³ Edmund Burke, *Selected Writings and Speeches*, 157.

¹⁴ *Ibid.*, 158.

¹⁵ Craig Nelson, *Thomas Paine: Enlightenment, Revolution, and the Birth of Modern Nations* (New York: Viking, 2006), 293.

¹⁶ J. F. C. Fuller, *Decisive Battles of the U.S.A.* (New York: Thomas Yoseloff, Inc., 1942), 33.

¹⁷ Fuller, *A Military History of the Western World*, Vol. II, 299.

¹⁸ Thomas Fleming, *Washington's Secret War: The Hidden History of Valley Forge* (New York: Smithsonian Books, 2005), 7.

¹⁹ Harlow Giles Unger, *Lafayette* (Hoboken, New Jersey: John Wiley and Sons, Inc., 2002), 43.

²⁰ James Thomas Flexner, *George Washington in the American Revolution (1775-1783)* (Boston: Little Brown and Company, 1968), 330-331.

²¹ Douglas Southall Freeman, *George Washington* (7 vols.; New York: Charles Scribner's Sons, 1951), IV, 115-120.

²² Richard B. Morris, *Witness at the Creation: Hamilton, Madison, Jay and the Constitution* (New York: Holt, Rinehart and Winston, 1985), 69.

²³ Catherine S. Crary, ed. *The Price of Loyalty: Tory Writings From the Revolutionary Era* (New York: McGraw-Hill Book Company, 1973), 148.

²⁴ *Ibid.*, 147, 149.

[25] Samuel Eliot Morison, *The Oxford History of the American People* (New York: Oxford University Press, 1965), 236.

[26] C-SPAN3 panel at the National Archives, taped September 12, 2004.

[27] North Callahan, *Flight from the Republic: The Tories of the American Revolution* (Indianapolis, Indiana: The Bobbs-Merrill Company, Inc., 1967), 34, 36, and 70.

[28] Morris, *Witness at the Creation: Hamilton, Madison, Jay and the Constitution*, 70.

[29] William Jay, *The Life of John Jay: With Selections From His Correspondence and Miscellaneous Papers* (Bridgewater, Virginia: American Foundation Publications, 2000), i, 47. Originally published in 1833.

[30] Freeman, *George Washington*, IV, 205.

[31] Paul Johnson, *A History of the American People* (New York: Harper Collins Publishers, 1997), 198.

[32] Walter Stahr, *John Jay*, 126, 193.

[33] Jay, *The Life of John Jay*, 69.

[34] McCullough, *John Adams*, 196; Stahr, *John Jay*, 91.

[35] Jay, *Correspondence and Public Papers*, iii, 114-115.

[36] Richard B. Morris, *The Forging of the Union 1781-1789* (New York: Harper and Row, Publishers, 1987), 61-62.

[37] *Ibid.*, 104.

[38] John Ferling, *A Leap in the Dark: The Struggle to Create the American* Republic (New York: Oxford University Press, 2003), 215-216.

[39] *Ibid.*, 210.

[40] *Ibid.*, 211-212.

[41] Richard B. Morris, *John Jay: The Winning of the Peace 1780-1784* (New York: Harper and Row, Publishers, 1980), 11.

End Notes: The Life of John Jay

⁴² McCullough, *John Adams*, 260-261.

⁴³ Jay, *Correspondence and Public Papers*, ii, 410.

⁴⁴ *Ibid.*, 411.

⁴⁵ *Ibid.*, 412.

⁴⁶ Walter Stahr, *John Jay,* 172-173.

⁴⁷ Jonathan R. Dull, *A Diplomatic History of the American Revolution* (New Haven, Connecticut: Yale University Press, 1985), 146.

⁴⁸ Richard B. Morris, *The Peacemakers: The Great Powers and American Independence* (New York: Harper and Row, Publishers, 1965), 300.

⁴⁹ Quoted in Robert Kagan, *Dangerous Nation* (New York: Alfred A. Knopf, 2006), 55.

⁵⁰ McCullough, *John Adams*, 279.

⁵¹ Morris, *The Peacemakers: The Great Powers and American Independence*, 459.

⁵² Forrest McDonald, *E Pluribus Unum* (Indianapolis, Indiana: Liberty Press, 1965), 144.

⁵³ Jay, *The Life of John Jay*, i, 198-199.

⁵⁴ Theodore Roosevelt, *The Works of Theodore Roosevelt*, Vol. IX: *The Winning of the West* (New York: Charles Scribner's Sons, 1926), 107.

⁵⁵ Jay, *The Life of John Jay*, i, 202-203.

⁵⁶ *Ibid.*, 239-240.

⁵⁷ John Rhodehamel, ed., *George Washington: Writings* (New York: The Library of America, 1997), 605.

⁵⁸ *Ibid.*, 643.

⁵⁹ John C. Miller, *Alexander Hamilton and the Growth of the New Nation* (New York: Harper Torchbooks, 1964), 152.

[60] Joseph J. Ellis, *Founding Brothers: The Revolutionary Generation* (New York: Vintage Books, 2000), 13.

[61] Russell Kirk, *The Conservative Constitution* (Washington, D.C.: Regnery Gateway, 1990), 43.

[62] Gary Scott Smith, ed. *God and Politics: Four Views on the Reformation of Civil Government* (Phillipsburg, N.J.: Presbyterian and Reformed Publishing Company, 1989), 223.

[63] Pat Robertson, *America's Dates with Destiny* (Nashville, Tenn.: Thomas Nelson Publishers, 1986), 92.

[64] Clarence B. Carson, *The Rebirth of Liberty: The Founding of the American Republic 1760-1800* (New Rochelle, N.Y.: Arlington House, 1973), 36.

[65] Rousas J. Rushdoony, *This Independent Republic: Studies in the Nature and Meaning of American History* (Nutley, New Jersey: The Craig Press, 1964), vii.

[66] Mark A. Noll, *A History of Christianity in the United States and Canada* (Grand Rapids, Michigan: William B. Eerdmans Company, 1992), 132.

[67] Harold O. J. Brown, *The Reconstruction of the Republic* (New Rochelle, N.Y.: Arlington House, Inc., 1977), 24.

[68] James C. Hefley, *America: One Nation Under God* (Wheaton, Ill.: Victor Books, 1975), 20.

[69] Peter Marshall and David Manuel, *The Light and the Glory* (Old Tappan, New Jersey: Fleming H. Revell Company, 1977), 284-285.

[70] Eidsmoe, *Christianity and the Constitution*, 138-143.

[71] *Ibid.*, 130-131.

[72] Gary North, *Political Polytheism: The Myth of Pluralism* (Tyler, Tex.: Institute for Christian Economics, 1989), 424-425.

End Notes: The Life of John Jay

[73] Francis Rufus Bellamy, *The Private Life of George Washington* (New York: Thomas Y. Crowell Company, 1951), 359.

[74] Holmes Alexander, *To Covet Honor: A Biography of Alexander Hamilton* (Belmont, Mass.: Western Islands, 1977), 10.

[75] James Thomas Flexner, *The Young Hamilton* (Boston: Little, Brown and Company, 1978), 436.

[76] Eidsmoe, *Christianity and the Constitution*, 157.

[77] Ellis, *Founding Brothers: The Revolutionary Generation*, 89-92.

[78] *Ibid.*, 110-111.

[79] Catherine Drinker Bowen, *Miracle at Philadelphia: The Story of the Constitutional Convention May to September 1787* (Boston: Little, Brown and Company, 1966), 201.

[80] *Ibid.*, 204.

[81] Jean Jacques Rousseau, *The Social Contract*, vol. 38 of *Great Books of the Western World*, editor-in-chief Robert Maynard Hutchins (Chicago: Encyclopedia Britannica, Inc., 1952), 396-397.

[82] *Ibid.*, 392.

[83] Quoted in Peter Viereck, *Conservatism: From John Adams to Churchill* (Princeton, New Jersey: D. Van Norstrand Company, Inc., 1956), 117.

[84] Sir Henry Sumner Maine, *Popular Government* (Indianapolis, Indiana: Liberty Classics, 1976), 66.

[85] *Ibid.*, 69.

[86] Alexander Hamilton, James Madison, and John Jay, *The Federalist Papers* (New York: Mentor, 1961, originally published in New York in 1788), 37.

[87] *Ibid.*, 38.

[88] Kevin Phillips, *The Cousin's Wars: Religion, Politics, and the Triumph of Anglo-America* (New York: Basic Books, 1999), 104, 224-228.

[89] Hamilton, Madison, and Jay, *The Federalist Papers*, 43.

[90] *Ibid.*, 43.

[91] *Ibid.*, 42, 45.

[92] *Ibid.*, 391.

[93] *Ibid.*

[94] Bruce Chadwick, *George Washington's War: The Forging of a Revolutionary Leader and the American Presidency* (Naperville, Illinois: Sourcebooks, Inc., 2004), 478.

[95] Monaghan, *John Jay: Defender of Liberty*, 1935, 312-313.

[96] Jay, *The Life of John Jay*, 285.

[97] *Ibid.*, 285-286.

[98] *Ibid.*, 287-288.

[99] Stahr, *John Jay*, 386.

[100] Jay, *Life of John Jay*, 216-217.

[101] Herbert Alan Johnson, *John Jay 1745-1829* (Albany, New York: New York State American Revolution Bicentennial Commission, 1976), 42.

[102] Jay, *The Life of John Jay*, 305-309, 316-320, 324-330; Kevin Belmonte, *Hero For Humanity: A Biography of William Wilberforce* (Colorado Springs, Colorado: NavPress, 2002), 172, 198, 199.

[103] *George Washington: Writings*, ed. by John Rhodehamel, 928.

[104] *Ibid.*, 950.

[105] Ellis, *Founding Brothers: The Revolutionary Generation*, 136.

End Notes: The Life of John Jay

[106] Walter McDougall, *Freedom Just Around the Corner: A New American History 1585-1828* (New York: Harper Collins Publishers, 2004), 354.

[107] Thomas Fleming, *Duel: Alexander Hamilton, Aaron Burr and the Future of America* (New York: Basic Books, 1999), 21.

[108] McCullough, *John Adams*, 456-457.

[109] Ron Chernow, *Alexander Hamilton* (New York: The Penguin Press, 2004), 486.

[110] John Lamberton Harper, *American Machiavelli: Alexander Hamilton and the Origins of U.S. Foreign Policy* (Cambridge, United Kingdom: Cambridge University Press, 2004), 150.

[111] Roosevelt, *The Winning of the West*, 418.

[112] Ferling, *A Leap in the Dark: The Struggle to Create the American Republic*, 378-379.

[113] Samuel Flagg Bemis, *Jay's Treaty: A Study in Commerce and Diplomacy* (New Haven: Connecticut: Yale University Press, 1962), 282, 287, 334.

[114] Richard Norton Smith, *Patriarch: George Washington and the New American Nation* (Boston: Houghton Mifflin Company, 1993), 232.

[115] Winston S. Churchill, *A History of the English-Speaking Peoples*, Vol. III: *The Age of Revolution* (London: Cassell and Company Ltd., 1957), 280.

[116] Chernow, *Alexander Hamilton*, 509.

[117] Eric Burns, *Infamous Scribblers: The Founding Fathers and the Rowdy Beginnings of American Journalism* (New York: PublicAffairs, 2006), 270-271.

[118] Jay, *The Life of John Jay*, 360.

[119] Stahr, *John Jay*, 337.

[120] Burns, *Infamous Scribblers*, 271.

[121] Monaghan, *John Jay: Defender of Liberty*, 422.

[122] Stahr, *John Jay*, 349.

[123] *Ibid.*

[124] *Ibid.*, 423.

[125] Jay, *Correspondence and Public Papers*, iv, 270-273.

[126] Miller, *Alexander Hamilton and the Growth of the New Nation*, 513-514. Richard Brookhiser, *Alexander Hamilton: American* (New York: The Free Press, 1999), 148, 152.

[127] Bruce Ackerman, *The Failure of the Founding Fathers: Jefferson, Marshall, and the Rise of Presidential Democracy* (Cambridge: Massachusetts: The Belknap Press of Harvard University Press, 2005), 124.

[128] *Ibid.*

[129] Jay, *Correspondence and Public Papers*, iv, 284-286.

[130] *Ibid.*, iii, 421.

[131] *Ibid.*, iv, 448.

[132] *Ibid.*, iv, 448-449.

[133] *Ibid.*, iv, 336.

[134] *Ibid.*, iii, 407.

[135] Stephen Budney, *William Jay: Abolitionist and Anticolonialist* (Westport, Connecticut: Praeger Publishers, 2005), 27-28.

End Notes: The Life of John Jay

PART II: The Character of John Jay

For as the body without the spirit is dead, so faith without works is dead also.[1]

In free states the laws alone bear rule; and, to that end, respect for and obedience to them is indispensable to the order, comfort, and security of society.[2]

Part II examines individually specific aspects of Jay's life. In some instances, mention was made of them in Part I, but now they are considered in the context of other related matters as each chapter is developed.

The Character of John Jay

The Bible

> *Let us therefore persevere steadfastly in distributing the Scriptures far and near, and without note or comment. We are assured that they "are profitable for doctrine, for reproof, for correction, for instruction in righteousness."[3]*

This is a good point to examine the Christian faith which underlay all that John Jay was. His faith was solidly evangelical, not rather vague as was that of Franklin and Jefferson, not rather general as was that of Washington, not subject to moral lapses as was that of Hamilton. Jay's faith and intellect did not clash; his intellect reinforced his faith. He was raised a member of the Church of England (after independence the Episcopal Church) during a time prior to the major challenges to the Biblical fundamentals of the faith within that body. He was committed firmly to belief in the Bible as the revelation of God. On May 12, 1825, he addressed to the American Bible Society the following:

> A merciful Providence also provided that some of these inspired men

should commit to writing such accounts of the Gospel, and of their acts and proceedings in preaching it, as would constitute and establish a standard whereby future preachers and generations might ascertain what they ought to believe and to do; and be thereby secured against the danger of being misled by the mistakes and corruptions incident to tradition. The Bible contains these writings, and exhibits such a connected series of the Divine revelations and dispensations respecting the present and future state of mankind, and so amply attested by internal and external evidence.[4]

Years earlier, he stated in a letter written to the Rev. Jedidiah Morse, a Congregationalist minister and a scholar in history and geography, that "It is to be regretted, but I so believe the fact to be, that except the Bible there is not a true history in the world."[5]

His faith shone brightly when his wife died on May 28, 1802, with Jay and their children at her bedside. After her passing, he led the grieving young people into the adjoining room and read to them 1 Corinthians 15 which presents the certainty of eternal life with Christ for those who are His. Although Jay's eyes were moist with sorrow over her death, his voice was firm due to the greater strength of his spiritual convictions.[6]

Frank Lambert rather badly missed the mark on Jay when discussing the religious beliefs of several significant figures in the early life of this country. He alleged that "among the Founders who rejected the faith of their Puritan Fathers for the Enlightenment were Franklin, Thomas Jefferson, Thomas Paine, John Adams, Alexander Hamilton, James Madison, and John Jay."[7] He later stated that "Franklin, Adams, Jefferson, Paine, Madison, Hamilton and Jay were unwilling to submit to the authority of any church's clergy, nor were they willing to accept uncritically the Bible as God's word."[8] Neither allegation is true of Jay who certainly was a believer in the Bible as divine revelation, nor could Alexander Hamilton be so described, especially when he returned to his faith more over the last years of his life. Of the others, although they were not orthodox believers, still the influence of the Christian world view was evident, particularly in the case of John Adams.

In 1821, Jay was elected president of the American Bible Society upon the death of Elias Boudinot. He wrote the secretary of the organization, the Rev. S. S. Woodhall, thanking them for the honor, setting forth his support for their purposes and goals, but considering his health not up to his properly fulfilling the duties of the office. The board sent two vice presidents to Bedford to assure Jay that no traveling would be required of him, that they would expect only that he deliver an annual address. With these stipulations, Jay accepted the election, serving until 1828, handling the correspondence expected of him and giving the annual address.

Faith

Enable me, merciful Father! to understand thy holy gospel aright, and to distinguish the doctrines thereof from erroneous expositions of them; and bless me with that fear of offending thee, which is the beginning of wisdom.[9]

The faith of John Jay went beyond being an intellectual assent to the truths revealed by God in the Bible; it also was heartfelt, something which permeated his whole being. The previously alluded to episode when, following the death of his wife, he read 1 Corinthians 15 to his children, was more than an affirmation of mind; it reflected a deep, personal faith in Jesus Christ as Savior and Lord.

Certainly Jay was a man with a well-developed intellect who did seek to understand as much as was possible that which he believed. He also was convinced that Christianity was the essential foundation of true civilization, as will be considered in other chapters. Here, though, our focus is on his personal faith. Jay was a rather reserved man, not outwardly demonstrative, so his Christian faith was not characterized by the emotional displays which exemplify the faith of many others. His feelings, though, including his Christian feelings, ran deep. When attempting to understand Jay, or anyone else, it is best to let that person speak for himself. Found among Jay's papers was an extensive prayer in his own hand. The following is part of it:

> Above all, I thank thee for thy mercy to our fallen race, as declared in thy holy gospel by thy beloved Son, "who gave himself a ransom for all." I thank thee for the gift of thy Holy Spirit, and for thy goodness in encouraging us all to ask it. I thank thee for the hope of remission of sins, of regeneration, and of life and happiness everlasting, through the merits and intercession of our Saviour, I thank thee for having admitted me into the covenant of this grace and mercy by baptism, for reminding me of its duties and privyleges, and for the influences of thy Holy Spirit with which thou hast favoured me.
>
> Let thy Holy Spirit purify me and unite me to my Saviour for ever, and

enable me to cleave unto him as unto my very life, as indeed he is. Perfect and confirm my faith, my trust, and hope of salvation in him and him only.[10]

It should be noted that Jay assuredly did not believe that Baptism in and of itself brings salvation. His statement in the above prayer was that Baptism brings the individual into a covenant relationship with God as did the Old Testament practice of male circumcision. Those who had gone through this, although they had been brought into the covenant, still could grow to adulthood, turn against God, and then be rejected by Him. So it is with those who have been baptized; they too can reject God. Unless they accept Christ as personal Savior and Lord, their Baptism counts for naught. Jay definitely was an evangelical Anglican, not high church.

This is a solid testimony of personal faith. No one has to scratch his head and wonder where Jay really stood spiritually. This was a living, vital faith which clearly seems to have lived in his life; inconsistencies did not appear between his profession and his practice. The Bible teaches that people "Should repent and turn to God, performing deeds appropriate to repentance."[11] This will serve as an introduction to Jay's Christian practice.

Christian Practice

Create in us all clean, and contrite, and thankful hearts, and renew within us a right spirit.[12]

Devout Christian he may have been, but Jay preferred to avoid religious disputation whenever possible. To illustrate, he argued against the proposal by William Cushing of Massachusetts that a prayer open Congress, maintaining that this would be divisive considering the number of denominations represented in the chamber. Samuel Adams, also of Massachusetts, suggested that since they were in Philadelphia, a clergyman of that city, the Anglican Jacob Duché, give the prayer. Adams stated that although he was of a different religious persuasion, he did not consider that an impediment since Duché was a good Christian and supported the colonial cause. This resulted in Duché's being chosen.[13] It does appear that Jay's concern was excessive, as would be proven by later experiences with clergy prayer at government functions and with chaplains in the military.

Furthermore, Jay made a point of not discussing his Christianity with those who were not in general agreement. For example, he and his wife were on cordial social terms with Benjamin Franklin. When, however, Franklin would begin to discuss his Deistic views, Jay would attempt to divert him, for instance by urging him to play his harmonica. Once, when a physician treating him started to scorn belief in a resurrection, Jay brought him to a grinding halt by snapping "Sir, I pay for your medical knowledge and not your distorted views of the Christian religion."[14]

These incidents and his general rule of not discussing religion with those who disagreed with him, could be attributed to a desire to avoid confrontation. That, though, was not consistent with his personality and record of taking strong stands, gentleman though he may have been. There often was a pattern of gentlemanly behavior which eschewed religious discussions in polite company. It might have been attributable to his belief in religious freedom or to a Calvinistic predestinarian tinge. At any rate, he gave many clear Christian testimonies during his long life and conducted himself in a manner congruent with his profession.

Jay's practice of Christianity was in line with his profession. He was a regular attendant at church services whose life was free of both public and private scandals. He was no more a perfect individual than any other human being, perfection not being a human attribute, but he well understood the Biblical admonitions concerning self-examination, repentance, and reform. Although firmly Anglican, he never was denominationally narrow and enjoyed fellowship with Christians of other persuasions, as exemplified by his attending a Presbyterian Church while in retirement at Bedford before an Episcopal parish was established there and by his serving as president of the American Bible Society. He raised his children, to quote Ephesians 6:4, in "the nurture and admonition of the Lord," and was blessed to see them, overall, turn out well. Customarily, he led family and guests in morning and evening devotionals and evening Bible reading. His son, William, wrote of him that "Mr. Jay's religion was fervent, but mild and unostentatious.... While his health permitted, he was regular in his attendance on public worship, and was always a scrupulous, but not superstitious observer of the Sabbath."[15]

The Character of John Jay

The Church

That duty, however, appears to me to call particularly on all ministers of the gospel, to look more to the Author and Finisher of our faith than to the expositors of it; and, disregarding the doubtful and mysterious doctrines by which the latter have divided Christians from Christians, to unite in defending the plain and intelligible faith delivered to us by our Redeemer and his apostles.[16]

With independence, the Church of England in the United States had to reorganize. During the colonial era, there were no bishops on this side of the Atlantic, partially because the Church had not yet developed the vision for an episcopate in the colonies and partially because no one had figured out how to support an American episcopate, especially in view of the number of non-Anglicans here. Under the circumstances, many Anglicans came to enjoy the greater freedom from not having an American bishop.

Now, though, changes had to come. Obviously, the Bishop of London could no longer exercise his jurisdiction, loose though it may have been.

Prayers for the monarch in the Book of Common Prayer had to be dropped. Since Loyalist sentiment was strong among the clergy, with the conclusion of the war many went into exile and had to be replaced. Indicative of this sentiment were the views of the Rev. Charles Inglis of New York who vehemently supported the British cause, particularly praising the Church of England clergy in New England, New York, and New Jersey for their steadfast adherence to their duty to their church and to their country in spite of being reviled and even physically attacked and jailed by independence supporters. Of the war, he stated that "The present Rebellion is certainly one of the most causeless, unprovoked and unnatural that ever disgraced any Country...."[17] In 1780, though, clergy and laymen who supported independence voted to call themselves the Protestant Episcopal Church, a name which subsequently came into general use for the national church.[18]

In particular, the new church had to secure bishops. In 1784, the Rev. Samuel Seabury was consecrated as the Bishop of Connecticut by the independent Church of Scotland since the Church of England still required that bishops take the oath of allegiance to the crown. A Church of England priest in Westchester County, New York, he had been a Loyalist during the late war. In the course of the

1776 campaign in New York, Jay had interrogated Seabury as part of the efforts to strengthen internal security. Expelled from his home, he served as a chaplain in a Loyalist regiment. After independence had been secured, he chose to become a citizen of the new United States. Jay opposed his consecration, partially because of wartime memories, partly because the high church Seabury advocated too strong an episcopacy.

Two years later, the Church of England dropped the oath of allegiance requirement; now the Archbishop of Canterbury or the Archbishop of York could consecrate bishops "without requiring them to take the oaths of allegiance and supremacy, and the oath of due obedience to the Archbishop...."[19] In 1787, the Rev. William White and the Rev. Samuel Provoost were consecrated as was the Rev. James Madison in 1790.* From then on, the Episcopal Church in the United States handled its own consecrations. During its early decades, the Church essentially was sound theologically. The Thirty-Nine Articles were made part of the original

---

* Provoost, assistant at Trinity Church, New York, before the war, had been an ardent supporter of independence and was more low church than Seabury. Jay heartily approved of him and supported his election as Bishop of New York. It should be noted that White and Madison also had been Patriots during the war for independence.

constitution of the Church in 1789. Only later in the nineteenth century would the inroads of liberal theology begin to erode that position, beginning a process which would culminate in the decision by the General Convention in 1988 to expunge the Articles from that document.

Although a committed Episcopalian, Jay did not hold to the high Anglican position that limited the definition of the Church to those which had the Apostolic Succession; he accepted the legitimacy of other denominations.[20] In retirement in Bedford, about thirty miles north of New York City, he attended a Presbyterian Church until an Episcopal parish was established. But, his Huguenot roots did surface in his animus toward Roman Catholicism, as was seen in his attempt, in effect, to disenfranchise Roman Catholics.

Christianity and Government

Certainly there would be little virtue in our civilization, and quite possibly there would exist no modern civilization at all, were it not for Christian preaching of the theological virtues.[21]

Among those who admire Jay, there are those who would have welcomed more outspokenness concerning his Christianity, especially in reference to a Christian foundation for the United States, comparable to the explicitly Christian statements in colonial charters and in state constitutions after independence. Also of concern was his frequent recourse to the term "popular sovereignty," words with overtones of Rousseau and the general will. Certainly as a devout Christian, Jay believed in the ultimate sovereignty of God, but sometimes there appeared a gap between his Christianity and the expression of his political thoughts, something all too common among others of the founding generation—a most remarkable aggregation in so many ways. Still, he did consider this to be a Christian country.* While serving as president

---

* For more information on this, the following books would be useful: Gary DeMar, *America's Christian History: The Untold*

of the American Bible Society, he referred in his 1822 annual address to the fact that "the conversion of the Gentiles is doubtless to be effected by the instrumentality of Christian nations...."[22]

In his study of government, as of everything else, Jay began with the Bible. Governments have been instituted by God to restrain evil which became part of the human condition subsequent to the Fall. He stated that:

> The depravity which mankind inherited from their first parents, introduced wickedness into the world. That wickedness rendered human government necessary to restrain the violence and injustice resulting from it.[23]

Concerning voting for those who reject Christianity, Jay presented a cogent warning based on Scripture in another letter to the Rev. Jedidiah Morse written on January 1, 1813:

Story (Powder Springs, Georgia: American Vision, Inc., 2000); John M. Pafford, *On the Solid Rock: Christianity and Public Policy* (LaGrange, California: Center for Cultural Leadership, 2003).

> Whether our religion permits Christians to vote for infidel rulers, is a question which merits more consideration than it seems yet to have generally received, either from the clergy or the laity. It appears to me, that what the prophet said to Jehoshaphat about his attachment to Ahab,* affords a salutary lesson on another interesting topic. [24]

While Jay was not really clear on a formal Christian foundation for this country, it certainly is apparent that he did not believe that Christians should vote for those who deny their beliefs and values lest they fall under the condemnation set forth in the reference to 2 Chronicles 19:2. It appeared to be his fervent hope that the United States, in effect, would be a Christian country.

Although, as was discussed earlier, the Constitution made no provision for an explicit spiritual foundation for the United States, this generally was done by the states, so people such as Jay were not too troubled by the omission. For example,

---

* "And Jehu, the son of Hanani, the seer, went out to meet him, and said to King Jehoshaphat, 'Shouldest thou help the wicked, and love them who hate the Lord?'" (2 Chronicles 19:2)

Article 22 of the 1776 Delaware Constitution stipulated that elected and appointed officeholders take the following oath:

> I _____, do profess faith in God the Father, and in Jesus Christ His only Son, and in the Holy Ghost, one God, blessed for evermore; and I do acknowledge the holy scriptures of the Old and New Testament to be given by divine inspiration.[25]

The Maryland Constitution, also adopted in 1776, set forth "That no other test or qualification ought to be required ... than such oath of support and fidelity to this State ... and a declaration of a belief in the Christian religion."[26]

The Massachusetts Constitution of 1780, in Chapter VI, Article I, required of everyone elected to state offices or to the legislature, the following oath: "I _____, do declare, that I believe the Christian religion, and have firm persuasion of its truth."[27]

Similar provisions were contained in other state constitutions of the period, giving some extenuation to those who did not push for something of this nature in the United States Constitution. In line with the conviction that this was a Christian country regardless of this omission, Joseph Story, Harvard Law School professor and Supreme Court justice from 1811 until his death in 1845, a man widely considered our preeminent constitutional scholar, stated that:

> Probably at the time of the adoption of the Constitution ... the general if not the universal sentiment in America was, that Christianity ought to receive encouragement from the State so far as was not incompatible with the private rights of conscience and freedom of religious worship. An attempt to level all religions, and to make it a matter of state policy to hold all in utter indifference, would have created universal disapprobation, if not universal indignation.[28]

While not a William Bradford nor a John Winthrop in terms of calling for a covenant relationship between this country and God, still among the major Founding Fathers, the Christian faith of John Jay was not surpassed.

The Character of John Jay

Principle and Party

The party for the constitution prevailed; and they have with as great unanimity approved of General Washington's civil as of his military measures and services. The party opposed to the constitution disapproved of the government established by it; and there are very few of the important measures of that government which have escaped their censure.[29]

Jay definitely was a committed Federalist, but he was not first and foremost a political party diehard; with him, principle always came ahead of party considerations. He was consistent in his conviction that party loyalty is not the highest good. Not often did he have to choose between what he saw to be right and what was in the best interests of the Federalist Party. There were, though, a couple of examples of his putting principle first.

While governor of New York, Jay had practiced this, keeping in office those Jeffersonians who proved to be honest, competent, and not clashing with his administration's goals. Of course party counted; he did consult with Federalist leaders such as Hamilton, but merit came first. His primary concern was for how well a man would do the job, not for how loyal a Federalist he might be. The caliber of his appointments was high, the eminent jurist and scholar James Kent being one of them.

As the state of New York gathered in 1820 for a constitutional convention, Jay spoke out for a spirit of inclusion in appointments to state offices. Since the Federalists had lost the electoral majority in New York as well as in most states with the exception of New England,* Jay, as a man dedicated to constitutional principles, did not disagree with the reality that the Democratic Republicans would control most governmental positions, but did appeal for at least a gesture to the Federalists, that they not be excluded totally. He stated that this should be done "instead of bestowing all upon men, recommended principally as ardent political champions, or as the noisy and active agents at our elections."[30]

An especially vivid example of Jay's putting principle above partisan considerations was his previously discussed resistance to Hamilton's scheme to undo the victory of Jefferson's party in

---

* By the end of the decade, the Federalist Party would be no more.

the 1800 presidential election. Washington had been unopposed the two times he ran for president. Behind the scenes, though, political parties had started to form. The Federalist leaders most prominent were Alexander Hamilton, John Adams, and John Jay. The opposition Democratic-Republicans rallied around Thomas Jefferson and James Madison. Washington sought to remain above the fray, but his convictions were on the Federalist side. The election of 1796 was bitterly contested between John Adams and Thomas Jefferson who finished in that order, Adams receiving seventy-one electoral votes, Jefferson sixty-eight. As the Constitution then stipulated, Jefferson, as the second place finisher, became vice president. The Federalists also controlled both houses of Congress. Bitter partisanship now would normally characterize American elections.

In the election of 1800, the Democratic-Republicans carried New York defeating the Federalists for control of the legislature which would select the state's presidential electors. Hamilton now sprang into action, urging Jay to convene the lame duck Federalist legislature to change the law concerning the choosing of these electors. Instead of being chosen by the legislature, they would be elected by popular vote by district. Were this to be done, Adams would have won enough votes in New

The Character of John Jay

York to win the Electoral College and be inaugurated in March 1801 to his second term.*

Certainly Hamilton's proposal was constitutionally permissible. Interestingly, the previous year Aaron Burr, to be Jefferson's vice president, proposed selecting electors by district when it appeared to favor his party. But now, to change the law after the election, although legal, rather obviously would have been, at the very least, morally questionable. As much as Jay did not want a Jefferson presidency, he did not even consider taking the action proposed by Hamilton; there was no possibility that Jay, a man of Christian integrity, would do something of this nature. He simply ignored the urging of his friend and political ally.

Hamilton, normally a man of public honesty, regarded the prospect of Jefferson's being president as catastrophic for the country because of his weak religious beliefs, his calling for limited central government power, and his having supported the French Revolution. Those concerns lay behind what certainly was not Hamilton's finest hour as he showed a darker side of the brilliance which he had used to such great effect in establishing this coun-

---

* Not until Franklin Delano Roosevelt began his second term in 1937 would the inauguration of the president be moved to January.

try on a solid economic footing. No such lapse afflicted Jay.

At this time, each elector cast two votes. The parties clearly had in mind one man for president, one for vice president. They organized their voting in the Electoral College so that their candidates for vice president would finish behind the candidates for president. They did this by having all electors cast one vote for the presidential choice and all but a few second ballots go to the vice presidential selection; the few thrown to other men ensured that there would not be a tie for first place.

But, in 1800 the Democratic-Republicans did not plan and organize effectively, so Jefferson and Burr received the same number of electoral votes. The determination of the next president now lay in the hands of the House of Representatives. Burr, obviously the party choice for vice president, refused to stand aside and maneuvered for the top position. For thirty-six ballots, neither man could secure victory. Finally, Hamilton who had considerable influence with Federalist representatives, threw his weight against Burr, a man he considered absolutely unprincipled, a worse choice than Jefferson and Thomas Jefferson now became our third president.

The Character of John Jay

Son and Sibling

A wise son heeds his father's instruction, but a scoffer does not listen to rebuke.[31]

Jay's father, Peter, married Mary Anna Van Cortland. They had seven children who survived to be adults. Both came from families of wealth and Peter's business ventures were very profitable, so the children were raised with many advantages, including educational opportunities. They were not, however, spoiled, pampered wastrels. Peter Jay was a firm but loving parent as was Mary, although less is known of her since none of her correspondence has been found. A number of Peter's letters can be read showing his interest in and concern for his progeny.

As the children grew, Mary Jay undertook the teaching of English grammar and Latin to them. It quickly became evident that young John had the intelligence and ability to learn evinced by his older brother, James. Of the other five siblings, Eve suffered from emotional difficulties, Augustus was retarded, and Peter[*] and Anna Maricka were

---

[*] Peter impressively overcame much of his handicap. As a youngster, he swam, fished, and climbed trees to find nuts.

blind due to smallpox. Frederick was normal with modest abilities. Although Frederick was involved in New York business undertakings and did serve in the New York Assembly, the bright lights of the family were James and John.

Before discussing relations between the siblings, it would be preferable to look further at the interaction between John and his father. Peter Jay's letters demonstrated a real love along with a determination to give clear, logical advice. He approved of John's interest in studying law. He wrote him, stating that "I hope you'll closely attend to it with a firm resolution that no difficulties in presenting that Study shall discourage you from applying very close to it, and if possible, from taking a delight in it."[32] This certainly was excellent advice. Firm resolution in the face of difficulties combined with an enjoyment of one's profession are a prescription for success. These characteristics already were evident in the still teen-aged John, but for someone so committed, fatherly advice was an encouragement and a reinforcement rather than nagging.

He developed an excellent memory. He farmed the family estate at Rye, showing skill at cultivating it and at judging and cattle. Furthermore, he could cover the estate alone on horseback. (Jay, *The Life of John Jay*, i, 450.)

As a sidelight, it is interesting to note that Peter addressed his son as "Johnny," an affectionate and informal approach. It also is of interest that his brother Frederick addressed him as "Jack." Apparently nicknames never caught on with John who did not use either when writing to his father and brother. He would show familial love, addressing Frederick as "My Dear Brother," and signing "Your very affectionate brother, John Jay." The touch of formality in the use of his full name was quite common at that time. He addressed his father as "Dear Sir" and signed "Your dutiful and affectionate son, John Jay."

Jay's combination of Christian love and sense of duty worked to make him an effectively caring son and brother. Both his parents had moved into their seventies as war broke out and spread to New York. In 1776 with beginning of fighting around New York City, he moved his parents and his wife up the Hudson River to Fish Kill which is north of West Point and south of Poughkeepsie. He made certain that they were provided for as their health failed. In 1777, Mary died, followed by Peter in 1782.

In terms of his relations with his brothers and sisters, Jay took responsibility for Augustus, who was retarded, and for Peter and Anna Maricka who were blind. He also in effect raised his nephew,

Peter Jay Munro, son of Eve whose Loyalist husband had left his family for the British side. Jay received little assistance from Frederick and James. Frederick possessed modest abilities and his success in business likewise was modest. He apparently was well meaning, but did little to lighten his brother's burdens. James was an entirely different matter. Possessed of a good mind, he graduated from King's College, studied medicine at Edinburgh, then the number one medical school in Europe, and became a member of the College of Physicians and Surgeons. His impressive fundraising for King's College earned him a knighthood from George III. As impressive as his achievements were, however, he seemingly felt surpassed by his younger brother and was not close or supportive. This attitude John did not reciprocate; he never showed any desire to get even. He would defend himself, but was not vindictive.

A strong-minded, determined man, Jay still was respectful and loving to his parents. He also stayed close to his brothers and sisters, with the exception that James on a number of occasions moved himself beyond the pale. In general, this was a good family without major rifts or petty cleavages. To this, Jay contributed much.

His Education

But if the mass culture, the democratic culture, becomes much alienated from the culture of the educated classes—why, presently the mass culture falls into decadence.[33]

In addition to family and church, education is a key factor in determining the character of the individual. Jay's parents intimately involved themselves with his education. His mother taught him English grammar and Latin, as she did the other children, although her working with the retarded Augustus was limited by his handicap. It quickly became evident that John was manifesting impressive intelligence and ability to learn, as had his older brother, James. Until he was eight, he was educated at home by private tutors. He then was enrolled in a grammar school (designed for boys generally from eight to about fourteen) headed by a Church of England priest, the Rev. Peter Stroupe. After three years there, he returned home to complete his preparation for college.

In 1760, John, now fourteen, entered King's College (now Columbia University) in New York City. It was grounded in the Church of England.

Trinity Church provided land for the institution, stipulating that the college president must be a communicant of the Church and chapel services would use the Book of Common Prayer. In addition, a majority of the board of trustees had to be Church of England members. A solid, rigorous classical education was provided for the students. This was exactly the type of college being sought by Peter Jay for both James and John—firmly Christian with an Anglican orientation and classical. It should be noted that students who were not Church of England members could attend Sunday services in their own churches.

Not only were academic standards high for the students at King's, so too were the entrance requirements. Before enrolling there, John had to demonstrate competence in Latin and Greek. One specific expectation was translating the first ten chapters of the Gospel of John from Greek into Latin. Another was to read the first three books of Virgil's *Aeneid*.

Education still was grounded in Christianity during the eighteenth century for both colleges and lower schools. The Enlightenment focus on secular education had not yet taken root in the British North American colonies. In the nineteenth century it would gain momentum, especially through the influence of John Dewey. Gradually publicly funded schools would push Christianity aside. Then, as a counter, parallel Christian education systems would arise in opposition to this development. At the time of Jay, however, education generally was Christian.

Furthermore, the curriculum at King's College was classical. Of course, people had to be familiar with what was going on around them, but the prevailing philosophy then was that studying history and great literature in Greek and Latin as well as in English and modern languages provided the best foundation for understanding the present. Not yet was education deeply infiltrated by the democratic dogma that everyone must be educated, that all should be in the same system. This pattern of thought would lead to the lowering of standards so that all could be accommodated happily.

Even though the academic environment at King's was serious, there were students whose off-campus activities ran to alcohol and women, there being a good number of bars and brothels in the city. In these pastimes Jay did not indulge. He certainly was not antisocial, but his moral principles were firm. Also his sense of responsibility and his ambition made him a serious student.

It is interesting to note that although from King's College came several key leaders in the struggle for independence, men such as Jay himself, Alexander Hamilton, Gouverneur Morris, and Robert Livingston, the full story is more complex. Actually, over half of the alumni were Loyalists, a percentage considerably higher than that of any other college in the colonies.[34] Keep in mind that a substantial proportion of Anglicans were loyal to the Crown.

Marriage

Who can find a virtuous wife? For her worth is far above rubies.[35]

A successful attorney of twenty-eight, Jay fell in love with Sarah Van Brugh Livingston, daughter of William Livingston, a prominent lawyer and future governor of New Jersey. She also was a distant cousin of Jay's former law partner, Robert Livingston. Informally known as Sally, she was the fourth of five lively, attractive daughters. The exact circumstances of their meeting are not known, but it most likely was at one of the social events frequented by people of the Jay and Livingston levels of society. Eleven years younger than her future husband, she was intelligent, sprightly, physically attractive, and more outgoing than John. She returned his love and accepted his proposal. They were married on April 28, 1774. Until her death in 1802, they were happy and passionately dedicated to each other. There is no indication that either ever strayed from the loving commitments they made to each other before God. They became the parents of two sons and four daughters, of whom more in the next chapter.

Sarah, a very fashionable lady, was an excellent hostess, a significant asset in John's rise. Of her, the sharp-tongued Abigail "Nabby" Adams, daughter of John and Abigail Adams, did say "Mrs. Jay dresses gaily and showily, but is very pleasing upon a slight acquaintance."[36] The rather catty opening did not detract from the compliment in the second part of the sentence, indicating the widespread appreciation for Sarah's graciousness and charm.

She also was a well-informed supporter of independence. She and John frequently discussed public matters and, perhaps not to the same extent as Abigail Adams, she gave her husband the benefit of her views. Their closeness was not merely domestic. There were, though, a few strains. When Jay was elected president of Congress, she learned of it from newspapers rather than from him directly. With an attempt at levity which only slightly concealed her concern about losing her closeness to John, she wrote to him that she could not emulate a Roman wife and see her husband absorbed in public life. Before she sent the letter, though, she received a missive from him to which she responded with words of love and pride in his accomplishments.[37]

When Jay went to Spain as minister plenipotentiary, she accompanied him, the only one of the American diplomats' wives to join her husband in Europe. This does not necessarily mean that they had a better marriage than, for example, John and Abigail Adams, but it clearly does indicate a deep bond, that they could not stand being physically parted for the years involved in his assignment. Her going with him also shows considerable toughness on her part, this journey being no easy move in the eighteenth century. The difficulty of the trip did deter other women and some men from wanting to undergo the hardships and dangers involved. At the time, they had only one child, Peter Augustus, who was just under three years old. He stayed with her family. During their European years, three children would be born to them, Susan (who died not long after birth), Maria, and Ann. Traveling with the Jays to Europe were Brookholst Livingston, Sarah's brother, and Peter Jay Munro, John's nephew, the son of his sister, Eve, and the Rev. Henry Munro, a Loyalist who had left his family.

The mutual respect between them was demonstrated by her decision to have their two daughters inoculated for smallpox in 1783 after the signing of the peace treaty between the United States and Britain. At the time, he was in London, she still in Paris. Inoculation worked, but people became sick from it, some dying, as did Jonathan

Edwards. There being danger in France at that time, she wrote John, but acted on her decision before receiving his concurrence. He did respond to her letter, completely approving of her action. As was standard with them, they were on the same page, each having trust in the judgment of the other.

When Jay was serving as chief justice of the United States Supreme Court, she traveled with him through New England while he heard cases for the eastern circuit.* Also with them was their son Peter, then fifteen. She did not, though, accompany him to London in 1794-95 when he headed the American delegation seeking to negotiate a treaty with the United Kingdom to establish normal relations between the two countries. The time of separation would be shorter than was involved in the earlier diplomatic service and the number of children for whom to care had grown. When they were separated, John wrote to Sarah at least once a week, sometimes more than one letter per day.

This was a good marriage between two Christian people who loved each other, trusted each other, were faithful to each other, had personalities

---

* See p. 131 for how the federal court system was organized and operated at this time.

which meshed well, complementing each other, and raised their children in the faith.

The Character of John Jay

As a Father

Train up a child in the way he should go, and when he is old he will not depart from it.[38]

John and Sarah Jay were the parents of six children: Peter Augustus (1776-1843): Susan (1780, died the same year); Maria (1782-1856); Ann, commonly called Nancy (1783-1856); William (1789-1858); and Sarah Louisa (1792-1818). As parents, they were dedicated to raising their sons and daughters in a loving, firmly Christian home. This can be seen in the way the children turned out and also is revealed in the letters Jay wrote during their times of separation.

As was typical for this time, the Jay girls were not as well educated as were the boys. Maria and Ann attended a girl's school in Bethlehem, Pennsylvania, Ann's stay, though, being cut short because of weak eyes; she returned home.

During the years she lived in Albany while her father was governor, Maria met Goldsborough Bayner, Jr., the son of an important political and business figure. Just after Jay left office in 1801, they were married and set up their home in Albany. After the death of her mother in 1802, Sarah

Louisa spent much of her time there as part of the household, although she did visit her father, siblings, and nieces and nephews in Bedford and New York City. Sarah would be a comfort to her older sister who suffered the death of one of her two sons shortly after his birth in 1804 and the death of her husband and other son in 1806. She continued to live in Albany for a number of years taking care of her aged father-in-law and sister, then moving to be near her father. Ann never left the nest, being with Jay until his death. The girls were loyal and dedicated, appreciating the love of their father even when he was stern with them.

The two boys also were the same. They both were men of substance and achievement, although not to the same degree as their father. Peter matriculated at Columbia College, as King's College, rather logically, had been renamed after the break with Britain. Jay, showing the same interest in his sons that his father had shown in him, wrote Peter advising him to study with care the lives of great men, recommending in particular the careful reading of Plutarch. Jay further called upon him to write his impressions on specific matters, such as examining Plutarch's segment on Cicero to ascertain "to what sets of indiscretion his misfortunes are to be ascribed."[39] Learning from the experiences of others is an important step on the path to wisdom.

Peter did well, graduating from his father's alma mater and commencing the study of law under his cousin, Peter Jay Munro. In many respects, John Jay had been a surrogate father for Munro. Before proceeding with his legal studies, though, young Peter took advantage of the opportunity to go to England as his father's private secretary during the negotiations for the 1794 treaty. This was an excellent opportunity for Peter to learn diplomacy from a master, witness significant international developments as an insider, and broaden his horizons through travel. Jay, no advocate for nor practitioner of nepotism, made certain that Peter knew what was expected of him and did his job conscientiously and effectively.

Back in the United States, Peter completed his law studies, passed the bar examination, and entered into law practice with Munro. Concerns that he may have contracted tuberculosis led to his spending a winter in southern Europe and another in Bermuda, but the worry was for naught. He recovered his health, married, fathered children, and became one of the most prominent attorneys in New York. He also handled his father's legal and business interests in New York City.

The most prominent of the Jay children was William, the second youngest. While living in Albany during his father's terms as governor, he began a lifelong friendship with James Fennimore Cooper. At the age of fifteen, he enrolled at Yale College, rather surprising considering the family ties to Columbia College/King's College. John Jay certainly was a traditionalist with a warm appreciation for his alma mater, but higher considerations now loomed larger. The Rev. Timothy Dwight, a Congregationalist, became president of Yale in 1795. He stepped into a situation where Deism had made substantial inroads into the student body. This he set about to correct, using reasoned arguments to turn the students back to the Bible and thence to faith in Christ as Savior and Lord. Dwight became one of the most significant leaders in the Second Great Awakening. His being a solid Federalist also contributed to the decision.

After graduation from Yale, William began law clerking in Albany, but weak eyes hit him just as the problem had afflicted his sister Ann. He returned to Bedford, married, and began a family. He served as a county judge, founded the American Bible Society, and became one of the most influential leaders in the abolition movement, albeit less known than he deserves. In 2005, a biography of him was published, somewhat making up for that.⁴⁰ He worked with his father on the Bedford interests and inherited the Bedford estate.

Although the quality of parenting is not reflected absolutely in how children turn out since individuals are responsible for their spiritual and moral states, still children who do well are a credit to their parents. As is stated in Proverbs 23:24: "The father of the righteous shall greatly rejoice...."

The Character of John Jay

Personality

Cheerfulness promotes health, and health promotes cheerfulness.... By indulgence, both cheerfulness and dejection will become habits, but of very different characters.[41]

The relationship between character and personality can appear to be rather tenuous. After all, an individual can be someone of high moral character, exhibiting integrity in all his or her dealings with others and be either an extrovert or an introvert. Still, though, over an extended period of time, the character of people will rise to the surface and show forth in their personalities. Shy, withdrawn people of good character will demonstrate it when engaged in interaction with others and weak character in those who are gregarious will become obvious. No matter what the personality, the virtues will dominate with the virtuous. Reserved people will take stands for what is good and right. Those who are outgoing also will focus on the good and the right, restraining tendencies to perform and center all on themselves. Different personality types face different challenges in the development of and demonstration of good character.

The Character of John Jay

Jay was reserved, sometimes appearing to be aloof, strait-laced, even supercilious. With family and friends, however, he could be relaxed, friendly, and let his sense of humor bubble to the surface. His humor could be sharp but not vicious. His physical appearance was in accord with his personality. He was tall, about six feet in height, slender. His portraits show a strong chin, sharp nose, and penetrating gaze. Intelligence and steadfastness also show forth in these portraits.

A conspicuous aspect of Jay's personality was his dedication to work conscientiously at the tasks for which he bore responsibility. On a number of occasions his health suffered as a result of too much work. For example, while practicing law before the outbreak of war, his health started to fail. His physician advised more exercise as essential if he wished to recover. He moved into quarters six miles from his office and rode into the city and back on horseback. The results were excellent.[42] Also, the intensity of the treaty negotiations in Paris in 1782 appears to have worn him down. On July 20, 1783, he wrote to Robert Morris, commenting on his health after the work on the treaty was over:

> My jaunt to Normandy did me some service, but less than I expected. The

pure air of this place has been useful to me. The pain in my breast has abated, and I have had no fever since I came here, which was about six weeks ago.[43]

On September 24 of the same year, in his letter to Gouverneur Morris (no relation to Robert), he remarked further on his health that:

The fact is, that my disorder has been gradually declining ever since I left the city [Paris]; but although the pain in my breast has diminished, it still continues, and daily tells me momento mori. As to the fever which the influenza left me, it has at last, thank God, taken its leave. During all my sickness, I have been happy in preserving a constant flow of spirits; and cheerfulness, that agreeable companion, has never forsaken me. I hope a trip to Bath will so patch up my "house of clay" as to render it tenantable a good while longer; a thorough repair I do not promise myself.[44]

The Character of John Jay

Here in these letters stand revealed several aspects of Jay's personality. Although he wrote to his friends of many different matters and did not exhibit obsessive preoccupation with his medical problems, still his health concerns did loom large. There well could be a psychosomatic aspect to some of his ailments. Of course, influenza is influenza, but some of his other complaints may be attributable more to stress than to purely physical causes. He demanded much of himself. Interesting too are Jay's dry sense of humor and patience concerning his difficulties combined with a determination to do all he could to improve his situation. Finally, his reference to the cheerfulness which never left him is praiseworthy. There must have been quite a few conflicts involving his faith and his common sense on the one hand and stress plus perhaps a tinge of hypochondria on the other. Jay, a man of faith, courage, and strength of character, rose above the second set of forces.

Even a cursory study of Jay's life shows his enjoyment of outdoor life, going back to his boyhood years at Rye, near Long Island Sound. In retirement at Bedford, he frequently was out on horseback before breakfast, another interesting segment of this complex man's personality.

Jay could be sensitive to slights and he could be stern, including with his family, something of which he was well aware, and made certain to show his love for them. He continually worked to temper the sometimes sharp edges of his personality. Here and in the earlier discussions are real tests of character, namely overcoming strong, negative sides of ones' personality. Everyone has some traits which he or she has to control, some inner fights which must be fought and won. After all, when there is no battle, there can be no victory. In general, the character of John Jay shone through his personality.

The Character of John Jay

Friendship

A man who has friends must himself be friendly, but there is a friend who sticks closer than a brother.[45]

Jay's being a friend to someone did not require that that person was in full accord with him. He had good personal relations with people who disagreed with him even on matters of Christian faith and on the battle for national independence. This did not mean that he was weak in his beliefs on either matter or that he was willing to compromise his convictions.

Although the Christian Jay had substantial theological differences with Benjamin Franklin, in general a Deist, and in spite of Jay's considering Franklin too much of a Francophile, still a sense of friendship rooted in respect was evident. In October of 1785, he wrote to Franklin who a few weeks earlier had returned to Philadelphia from France. Pennsylvania now elected him president (the title then used) of the state. Jay commented upon the honor done Franklin and the widespread esteem in which he was held. He then expressed joy at learning of Franklin's plans to visit New York. He averred that:

> Mrs. Jay is exceedingly pleased with this idea, and sincerely joins with me in wishing to see it realized. Her attachments are strong, and that to you being founded in esteem and the recollection of kind offices, is particularly so.[46]

During the war, Jay's good friend, fellow King's College alumnus, and fellow attorney, Peter Van Schaack, was a loyalist; he refused to take an oath of allegiance to the United States and was sent into exile. In spite of this sharp divergence, their friendship survived. While Jay was serving on the Peace Commission in Paris, he received a letter from Van Schaack, dated August 11, 1782, written from London. In it, he wrote of the reality that they were on different sides, but continued:

> Whether what has passed has altered your opinion of me as a man, I own, is a question I could wish to have resolved. The artificial relations, introduced by a state of society, may vary or be dissolved by events and

external circumstances; but there are others which nothing but deviation from moral rectitude can, I think, annihilate.[47]

To this reaching out, Jay responded clearly that:

No man can serve two masters: either Britain was right and America wrong; or America was right, and Britain wrong.... Hence it became our duty to take one side or the other; and no man is to be blamed from preferring the one which his reason recommends as the most just and virtuous.[48]

But, concerning their friendship, Jay assured Van Schaack that:

Your judgment, and consequently your conscience, differed from mine on a very important question; but though, as an independent American, I considered all who were not for us, and you among the rest, as against us; yet be assured that John Jay did not cease to be a friend to Peter Van Schaack.[49]

The Character of John Jay

With the end of the war and the signing of the Treaty of Paris, Van Schaack decided to accept the changed circumstances and return to his home. Jay intervened to smooth the way for him.

Another interesting study of friendship in Jay's life is his handling of the call by Alexander Hamilton to organize the reversal of Thomas Jefferson's electoral victory of 1800 through political sleight of hand in New York.* Although Jay and Hamilton were political allies and friends, Jay's sense of what is right proved stronger; distasteful as Jefferson's election was to him, he would not sacrifice his integrity.

Another intriguing friendship was that between Jay and Gouverneur Morris, a man of great intelligence and ability. This he had in common with Jay. Morris, though, was rather a roué; his reputation as a ladies' man was widely known. This Jay never was; no breath of sexual scandal ever wafted up out of his life. They were, however, friends with respect for each other's good points and with genuine affection for each other. In fact, in 1813, the mature Morris asked Jay to be one of the godfathers for his newborn son, stating that "Should you be mingled with the dust, he shall learn from the history of your life, that a man must

---

* See chapter above, "Principle and Party."

be truly pious to be truly great."[50] Morris, a believer in religious toleration, had a respect for the faith of Jay, even though he did not evince anything close to his Biblical faith. In spite of this lack of fundamental accord, Morris had a high regard for the sterling qualities of Jay, even though he chose not to practice many of them himself.

Jay was not one to drop friends when trouble arose, nor to betray them when it looked as if he might gain from doing so. Nor would he put friendship above higher considerations and follow his friends into actions which violated his Christian beliefs. He well understood the admonition in James 4:4: "Do you not know that friendship with the world [that is, with the world system as against that of God] is enmity with God?" Jay's life provides lessons for being a Christian friend; loyalty and dependability to others, but always within the context of higher principles.

The Character of John Jay

Courage

Be strong and of good courage, do not fear nor be afraid of them; for the Lord your God, He is the one who goes with you. He will not leave you nor forsake you.[51]

On frequent occasions, Jay demonstrated physical and moral courage. Although he did not see combat duty during the war, there were times of threat to life and limb. First of all and most significant was the distinct possibility of execution for treason were the cause of independence to lose. Jay, one of the most prominent leaders of the new country, would have been high on any list of those to suffer death for treason to the Crown.

Very specific and more immediate threats to Jay's life were involved in his 1779 trip to Spain after being chosen by Congress to serve as the American minister to Spain. He and his party sailed from Philadelphia in late October, a notoriously dangerous time of year to cross the North Atlantic. They traveled on the Confederacy, a thirty-two gun frigate. On November 7, the ship was struck by a ferocious storm which knocked down all three masts and damaged the rudder. The danger of foundering was great, but the crew set up a makeshift mast and made temporary repairs to the rudder, sufficient to steer the ship. The battered vessel also would have been unable to maneuver were a British warship to encounter them and would have been sunk or captured. Finally, the Confederacy limped into port at the French West Indian island of Martinique. Through all this time of peril, Jay remained calm, proving his courage when facing situations of hazard.

Moral courage too characterized Jay's pattern of life. Standing up for what one believes when confronting the loss of friends, income and opportunities while at the same time being subjected to vicious attacks and ridicule, certainly requires great courage. The temptation is there to cut corners, to shade things to avoid the above consequences. For example, in Paris as part of the American delegation negotiating independence and peace with the British, Jay, for a time, stood alone. John Adams had not yet arrived, Benjamin Franklin was ill, and John Laurens had been captured and imprisoned by the British when his ship was seized during the Atlantic crossing. Jay insisted that the British acknowledge at the start of the talks that they were dealing with an independent country. The French and some of his colleagues considered this too demanding, that his stance could close the door to negotiations before they even began. Recognition of American independence, they believed, should be part of the treaty to be drawn up. To Jay, a serious principle was involved—we already were the United States of America, not just a group of rebellious colonies. Jay stayed firm in spite of opposition and the British conceded the point.

Jay appreciated French aid, understood how significant it was in helping the United States to win. But, he recognized that the primary motivation of the French government was to get back at the British who had defeated them in the Seven Years War. Of course, individuals such as Lafayette genuinely supported the American cause, but the government in Paris would sacrifice American interests if that would benefit France. Although Adams too distrusted French intentions, Franklin was strongly pro-French as were many other Americans such as Thomas Jefferson. There in Paris, Jay was subject to many overt and subtle French influences and had to be clear-sighted, firm in his responsibilities as an American representative, and courageous in word and action. He succeeded admirably in each.

The treaty with Britain in 1794, commonly known as Jay's Treaty, brought great recriminations on Jay's head; he even was burned in effigy.

The Character of John Jay

As was discussed, most historians regard this as the best we could have done considering our military weakness at that time, that, in addition, there were economic advantages for the United States. By 1794, Jay had served as chief justice of the New York Supreme Court, president of Congress, minister to Spain, member of the Peace Commission, secretary of foreign affairs, and presently was chief justice of the United States Supreme Court. He was considered one of the foremost contenders to succeed George Washington as president. He had many supporters for his treaty efforts and, by and large, has been vindicated by historians. Still, though, he was attacked harshly and became so controversial that the Federalists chose John Adams as their candidate. Adams might have won anyway, but whatever chance Jay had was lost. He did what he believed was right, was best for the country, and accepted the consequences.

Jay's call for the abolition of slavery, discussed in another chapter, was supported by many of his fellow Americans, but was opposed by others who either wanted to continue slavery or who wanted to avoid any consideration of the issue. His principled stand was another example of moral courage.

It is not often easy to do what is right. Many times throughout his life, Jay faced crossroads situations when courage was required to do the right thing. He did not fail.

The Character of John Jay

Professional Life

In free states the laws alone bear rule; and, to that end, respect for and obedience to them is indispensable to the order, comfort, and security of society.[52]

Jay graduated from King's College with a thorough and classical education. His months clerking and reading the law in Benjamin Kissam's office provided him with both a theoretical and a practical knowledge of law and the legal profession. He carried into his profession traits already well developed; his integrity and his work ethic were rooted in his Christianity, indeed, they were demonstrations of that faith. He had a deep love of the law, of the belief that countries must be governed by settled law rooted in God's revelation. Jay wrote to a friend in 1818 that "The moral or natural law was given by the Sovereign of the universe to all mankind...."[53] He later wrote in the same letter some of God's positive ordinances were not for all at all times, such as circumcision. Others, though, are unchanging. For example, he wrote that "The punishment for murder has undergone no alteration, either by Moses or by Christ."[54]

The Character of John Jay

Often, Jay evinced a punctilious concern for adhering strictly to proper procedure even when others were willing to slide around the edges, avoiding being precise. For example, his stand in the previously discussed dispute at King's College appeared finicky and unreasonable to the administration there and his demanding British recognition of our independence prior to beginning negotiations seemed too exacting. Yet to Jay, clear-cut principles were involved in each case and he stood his ground.

This same determination to be precise was revealed in his service as clerk of the royal boundary commission charged to adjudicate the border dispute between New York and New Jersey in 1769. The commission did its job, drawing the line between the provinces. Acceptance by the two parties was rather slow; in 1772, the assemblies of the provinces approved the settlement. Governor William Tryon of New York and Governor William Franklin (Benjamin's son) of New Jersey also supported the new boundary. But, at this stage, Jay refused to release the transcript of the commission's deliberations. His reason may have been connected to his not having been paid for his services as clerk. Probably more significant was the absence of any official sanction for him to do so. In

February 1773, the New York legislature passed a special bill authorizing his release of the records.[55]

By this time, Jay had established himself at the top of the legal profession in New York in terms of both prestige and income; in fact, he was starting to become known to those beyond the borders of his home province. In August 1774, John Adams, passing through New York on his way to Philadelphia, wrote of Jay's having been described to him as "a hard student and a good speaker."[56] Of course, much higher praise was to come, but the words from Adams were a beginning.

Jay always was a man of honor in the legal profession as he was in all areas of his life. Still, he was not naïve, a Pollyanna blind to the reality of the evil which confronts and opposes those who seek to do good. In 1770, he wrote to a friend that "The duplicity and disingenuousness which shades the character of many about me daily remind me of the openness and sincerity of my absent friend."[57] Jay was an excellent example of the admonition given by Christ recorded in Matthew 10:16 to be "wise as serpents, and harmless as doves." He functioned powerfully and effectively in this world, encountered evil daily, but neither withdrew from active life nor was he drawn away from his Christianity.

Those who are good stewards of what God has entrusted to them dedicate themselves to His service and develop their talents and opportunities to the highest degree possible. This includes their professional lives; being the best they can in their professions is a very significant facet in their honoring God. By becoming an outstanding lawyer in the private sector and by serving with honor and ability in the public sector, John Jay showed his Christianity; his works demonstrated his faith as we are taught in James 2:17-18:

> Even so faith, if it has no works is dead, being by itself.
>
> But someone may well say, "You have faith and I have works: show me your faith without the works, and I will show you my faith by my works."

John Jay's Christianity was not compartmentalized; it permeated all that he was and all that he did.

Power and Authority

Conviction that civilized society requires orders and classes, as against the notion of a "classless society...." If natural distinctions are effaced among men, oligarchs fill the vacuum.[58]

Power is held as a trust by those in authority, to be used for the benefit of all, not for the exclusive gain of those who exercise it. This John Jay believed and practiced. He was a sterling example of a solid conservative, not just in eighteenth century terms; there are people like him today and have been throughout the history of this country. He was committed to the establishment of a country with order, justice, and freedom under God. These last two words are essential in order to understand his views on power and authority. Everything begins with God; His power and authority are supreme. Within this context, Jay believed in government responsible to the people who express their opinions through free elections. He was a republican rather than a democrat, meaning that he wanted a system of government in which the voters elect those who govern; they do not govern directly themselves, but rather through their elected representatives.

Jay was not an advocate of universal suffrage, but averred that the capable should be the ones voting and serving in office. This did not mean those born at a certain level of society, but rather those who rose based on their abilities and their achievements. This concept of a "natural aristocracy" was shared by others such as John Adams and Alexander Hamilton, men born into lower strata of society than Jay, but who rose to positions of significance and leadership because of their talents. Jay may have been born into privilege, but this was not his criterion of judgment. His importance was based on his accomplishments, not on an accident of birth. On this topic, John Adams commented:

> The nobles have been essential parties in the preservation of liberty...against kings and people... By nobles, I mean not peculiarly an hereditary nobility, or any particular modification, but the natural and actual aristocracy among mankind.... The numbers of men in all ages have preferred ease, slumber, and good cheer to liberty.... We must not, then, depend alone upon the love

> of liberty in the soul of man for its preservation.... When the people who have no property feel the power in their own hands to determine all questions by a majority, they ever will attack those who have property.... The multitudes, therefore, as well as the nobles, must have a check.[59]

Jay himself said it well in a letter to William Wilberforce:

> But I have observed nothing in it [the English Constitution] which even implies what is called "universal suffrage." It is not a new remark, that they who own the country are the most fit persons to participate in the government of it. This remark, with certain restrictions and exceptions, has force in it; and applies both to the elected and the electors, though with most force to the former.
>
> The French revolution has so discredited democracy, and it has so few influential advocates in Europe, that I doubt its giving you much more trou-

ble. On the contrary, there seems to be a danger of depreciating it too much. Without a portion of it there can be no free government.[60]

Jay was well aware, as were the wisest Founding Fathers such as Washington, Hamilton, John Adams, and Gouverneur Morris, of the threats to freedom from a ruler whose power is unchecked, from the majority which, if unchecked, can ride roughshod over the capable and productive, and the capable and productive who, if unchecked, can oppress the masses. Hence, Jay's support for the United States Constitution which by providing for a President, a House of Representatives, and a Senate recognized the monarchical, democratic and aristocratic elements, balancing them and doing the best humanly possible to preclude having any one grind the others under its heel.

Jay's Christianity was foundational, so he rejected the core principle of democratic philosophy that the people are the ultimate sovereign, that is, the highest standard of good and truth. If the people are sovereign, then God cannot be; there can be only one source from whence flows all that is good and true. If the people are sovereign, then the Israelites were right when they abandoned God to worship a golden calf while Moses and Joshua had gone to Mount Sinai where Moses received from God the Ten Commandments.[61] After all, the decision to worship the idol was sanctioned by the majority. If democratic philosophy is correct, never mind what God has revealed to us, the majority determination prevails. As was trenchantly stated by Lord Percy of Newcastle, a wise mid-twentieth century Englishman, "The first and fundamental characteristic of democracy is that it is an exclusive religion."[62]

      This was not the thinking of Jay. He did believe in individual freedom and in the right of the people to determine the course of their lives. But, this must not be unlimited, unchecked power. The minority, which throughout history has been innovative, entrepreneurial, and productive is entitled to freedom from majority use of the political process to tear them down and expropriate the fruits of their labor. Some taxation is needed to support some government, but both must be limited. Above all, human power and authority are subordinate to God and subject to His Commandments.

The Character of John Jay

Loyalty and Revolution

What reason is there to expect that Heaven will help those who refuse to help themselves; or that Providence will grant liberty to those who want courage to defend it.[63]

Jay was among the last of the key Founding Fathers to conclude that a break with Britain was necessary if the colonists in North America were to enjoy the blessings of justice and freedom. His father and brothers came to back independence earlier than did he. His preference had been to stay loyal to the Crown. As a believer in justice and freedom, he had been repelled by the high-handed actions of the British government toward the North American colonies as exemplified by the Stamp Act and the Intolerable Acts. As a supporter of order too, however, he rejected the mob actions of some colonists as a legitimate response to the grievances they suffered. He wanted reform, but within the British system. Jay was by no means a firebrand for independence such as Samuel Adams or Thomas Paine. He became a revolutionary by force of circumstances, not by first choice or by temperament. Reason and persuasion were to be used first, then trade sanctions if necessary. A war for independence would be the last resort.

As a member of the Continental Congress, Jay worked assiduously for orderly reform of the system from within. New York was sharply divided, many agreeing with Jay, others regarding this position as beyond any prospect for success and were ready to break away immediately.

In September 1774, Jay wrote the "Address to the People of Great Britain" which was endorsed by Congress the same month. He set forth the contention that the colonists were entitled to all the traditional rights of freeborn Englishmen. Furthermore, Jay charged that the British Parliament was overstepping its rightful powers with the acts it had passed against the colonists. Arguing for these traditional rights and later fighting for them was the hallmark of those who built this country. These were concrete rights which governments should protect, not vague, utopian musings of philosophers.

A resolute conservative, he was dedicated to a society based on order, justice, and freedom—in that sequence. He abhorred mob rule and supported precedence and tradition, hence his wanting the colonies to stay loyal parts of the realm. He labored valiantly with others such as John Dickenson and Joseph Galloway to hold everything together. Galloway proposed the setting up of an American Parliament which would have power equal to the British Parliament and which could block the imposition of dictates from London. Support for staying within the Empire was fading, though, and Galloway's hope failed passage by just one vote.

Later Jay put forward the "Olive Branch Petition," seconded by Dickinson, to seek a better deal for the colonies short of independence. It passed with support from those convinced a break with Britain was necessary because they believed that the government in London would prove to be intransigent and that those still optimistic about change within the system would be convinced that their course no longer had any chance of success. In this they were right. British refusal to consider a reasonable course of action and the outbreak of war convinced him that advocacy of independence was the better course for anyone believing as he did in justice and freedom in addition to order.

Jay supported settled government operating within a constitutional framework—key aspects of British polity. His deeply held principles now mandated separation. Once he made this decision, he did not look back, did not second-guess himself, and wholeheartedly served his new country to the best of his ability. For the new United States, Jay labored with dedication and effectiveness to bring into being a government which would establish order, promote justice, and protect freedom. He was a loyal and patriotic American, but above all, he was a man committed to abiding principles which transcend national boundaries. After his decision to support independence, Jay never faced any conflict between his loyalty to principle and his loyalty to the United States.

War and Peace

As, therefore, Divine ordinances did authorize just war—as those ordinances were necessarily consistent with the moral law, and as the moral law is incorporated in the Christian dispensation, I think it follows, that the right to wage just and necessary war is admitted, and not abolished by the gospel.[64]

Although not a highly martial type of man such as George Patton, Jay did support war when the alternatives were unquestionably worse. He was given a commission as a colonel in the New York militia, but he did not serve on active duty. As the New York area became the primary theater of the war, Jay provided effective leadership in setting up a spy network in British held territory and in counter-intelligence actions. In addition, he led an expedition to procure cannons to fortify the heights at West Point, blocking the British from further penetration up the Hudson River. Jay was no pacifist. He did try to find a peaceful solution to the troubles with Britain, but once it became clear that no reasonableness was coming forth from the

British government, Jay wholeheartedly supported war as the only reasonable option for the colonies.

Jay's attitude toward war when circumstances necessitated strong action was shown in his report to the president of Congress on October 13, 1785 while he was serving as secretary of foreign affairs. In it, he commented on the prospect of war with Algeria over the seizure of American citizens and ships. He believed that aggression against the United States would unify Americans and could serve to galvanize our people in support of a strong navy. In response to the call for suggestions on how to implement his points, Jay called for arming at government expense American merchant ships trading in the Mediterranean and the building of five forty gun ships.[65] This was not done then as the weak government under the Articles of Confederation did not act. In a few years, under the new Constitution, effective action would be taken against the North African (Barbary) states.

Jay's interest in matters of national defense continued. While serving as chief justice of the United States Supreme Court, he wrote President Washington on November 13, 1790 a missive dealing with a number of constitutional issues. In it, he gave his views on some specific defense considerations.

It appears advisable, that the United States should have a fortress near the heads of the western waters; perhaps at, or not very distant from Fort Pitt, to secure the communication between the western and Atlantic countries; and that the place be such as would cover the building of vessels proper for the navigation of the most important of those waters. Should not West Point, or a better post if to be found on Hudson River, be kept up? An impregnable harbour in the north, and another in the south, seem to me desirable. Peace is the time to prepare for defense against hostilities.[66]

Later, while governor of New York, Jay continued to concern himself with military affairs. The United States in the late 1790s was engaged in an undeclared conflict with the new revolutionary government of France. The possibility was there for a major war to develop. John Adams, then president, sought to avoid war and did succeed in doing so, but prepared for the worst. If war were to break out, George Washington, called out of retirement at Mount Vernon, would command, but due to his growing infirmity, would not actively lead the army in the field. Alexander Hamilton, designated inspector general, would do so. On August 30, 1798, Jay wrote Hamilton getting New York ready for war and suggesting how to handle certain operational details. In the letter he stated that:

> There are several topics on which I wish to converse with you, and particularly respecting military arrangements at New York. The rifle corps, and a few of the new light infantry companies are established. There were reasons which I shall mention when we meet, which induced me to suspend a decision relative to the others for the present.... The defense of the port, etc., in my opinion, should be under your direction. The measures will be concerted between us.[67]

Again, these measures were not needed, but Jay was acting responsibly as governor, preparing for all contingencies. Such common sense he showed in national and state office.

A country which wishes to be free, peaceful, and strong has many considerations with which to deal, not the least of which is defense against those who wish it ill. Jay's statement in the previously quoted letter to President Washington that "Peace is the time to prepare for defense against hostilities" is accurate and profound, well worth being committed to memory by all Americans, especially those in positions of leadership. All too often, peace breeds complacency as many assume peace is natural and permanent and we then find ourselves poorly prepared when forced to fight for freedom. Once again, John Jay proved himself a man of principle who was rooted in reality. In times of challenge, the United States has been blessed by God with people such as Jay, the type of leader who does not seek conflict, but who does not shrink from fighting when necessary to preserve order, justice, and freedom.

The Character of John Jay

Slavery

As to my sentiments and conduct relative to the abolition of slavery, the fact is this:—In my opinion every man, of colour and description, has a natural right to freedom, and I shall ever acknowledge myself to be an advocate for the manumission of slaves....[68]

Slavery, although concentrated in the South and generally associated with that region, was found in all parts of the country. Jay's family and Jay himself held slaves, although his attitude was to undergo a sharp transformation; it is not definite when this change took place, but it certainly had taken place by the time of the Declaration of Independence. Shortly after Congress had approved the Declaration, Jay was selected to chair a committee to draft a state constitution. By the spring of 1777, they had completed their task. He supported the efforts by Gouverneur Morris for the gradual ending of slavery in New York. The convention, however, did not pass the measure.

By this time, Jay most assuredly opposed slavery and called for its abolition. He wished the emancipation process to be gradual, however, so that the former slaves would be prepared for the responsibilities of freedom. He wanted to avoid the chaos which would ensue if a mass of people without experience in freedom and with few marketable skills suddenly appeared in our midst. Jay advocated freedom, but freedom within a framework based on order and justice; only then could it flourish. He had to combat those who wanted no change, believing that slavery was economically needed and/or the societal consequences of emancipation would be catastrophic. In addition, there were some who called for the immediate ending of slavery, regardless of the effects of that action.

In line with his gradualist philosophy of emancipation was his purchase of a slave in Martinique and his providing for his freedom five years later. Jay and his party had stopped at the French island on their way to Spain in 1779. His viewing of the harsh treatment of slaves on the sugar plantations filled him with aversion. He was, though, impressed by the appearance and demeanor of a fifteen year old slave named Benoit. Jay purchased him to be his personal attendant, a better fate than what probably lay ahead were he to remain a slave on Martinique. Consistent with his convictions, in 1784 Jay freed Benoit with the freedom to take effect after three more years of service. Benoit's status with Jay was more that of an employee than a slave. Walter Stahr, in his overall excellent biography of Jay, concluded that Jay's document of manumission was not particularly impressive: "Like Jay's attitudes towards slavery, the document is contradictory: it recognized the injustice of slavery in general, but required Benoit to serve Jay for another three years."[69] He was dedicated to the extirpation of slavery, but in an orderly, organized manner. Benoit would serve three more years to at least partially repay Jay for the money spent on him. One can disagree with the tactics advocated by Jay for ending slavery, but his dedication to the cause cannot with justice be questioned.

In 1785, Jay was an active leader in the founding of the New York Manumission Society. Also involved with him were such prominent New Yorkers as Alexander Hamilton, Philip Schuyler, and Robert Livingston. At its first meeting, the organization elected Jay president. Initially, it looked as if they were going to be successful in having enacted by the New York legislature a bill for gradual emancipation along the lines of what had passed in Pennsylvania. Various machinations doomed the prospects for passage at that time. Final success would have to wait until 1799 when Jay was governor of the state.

While in England negotiating the 1794 treaty, Jay met and developed a warm friendship with

William Wilberforce. They shared an evangelical Christian faith, Anglicanism, and a firm determination to end the scourge of slavery. They discussed and later wrote each other about their efforts to stop the slave trade and then slavery itself. Also, neither had the bitterness toward the country of the other that characterized too many of their countrymen. Jay certainly supported American independence, but he understood that our political and judicial principles were British in origin. In one of his letters to Wilberforce, written November 8, 1809, he expressed his appreciation for the efforts of the abolitionists in Britain and for the beneficial influence of Britain around the world:

> It is pleasing to behold a nation assiduously cultivating the arts of peace and humanity in the midst of war [against Napoleon], and while strenuously fighting for their all, kindly extending the blessings of Christianity and civilization to distant countries.[70]

In 1795, Jay was elected to the first of his two terms as governor of New York. Now he occupied an executive position from which he could influence events in the state. One of the problems in ending slavery was that no acceptable plan had been devised to reimburse slave owners for the freed slaves. In April 1799, a law supported by Jay was passed by the New York legislature which provided for all offspring born to slaves after July 4, a very symbolic choice, would be free. In order to ensure that they would be ready for being constructive free citizens, men would serve apprenticeships until they were twenty-eight, women until twenty-five. The law also forbade the exporting of slaves.

His interest in the abolition of slavery continued, as evinced by his continued support of the New York Manumission Society and his correspondence with William Wilberforce. Another indication of this ongoing commitment to change was his being part of the establishment of the New York School for Free Africans, showing his determination to aid in preparing former slaves to be constructive free citizens. At Bedford, he employed several former slaves and had one slave not yet ready for freedom. Once more demonstrated in these activities was his belief in gradual emancipation with the freed slaves ready for freedom.

In this long fight for a clear principle, Jay was persistent, not deterred by opposition or setbacks, firm in his determination to succeed.

The Character of John Jay

Indians

There is neither Greek nor Jew, circumcised nor uncircumcised, barbarian, Scythian, slave nor free, but Christ is all and in all.[71]

In the 18th century, the most powerful aggregation of Eastern Woodland Indians was the Iroquois Confederacy. It had been established in the middle of the 16th century, initially comprising five tribes, the Seneca, the Cayuga, the Onondaga, the Oneida, and the Mohawk. In 1722, the Tuscarora joined. Militarily it was a force with which to be reckoned. Savage warriors, they were known for striking long distances and for torturing those prisoners they decided not to adopt. Their territory extended from western Massachusetts and Connecticut in the east to western New York and from the St. Lawrence River in the north to the Susquehanna in the south.

In the wars between the British and the French, most of them sided with the British, although some who had converted to Roman Catholicism, mostly Mohawks and Onondagas, took the other side. During the American Revolution the majority of the Iroquois were allied with the

British. Initially, it appeared as if the Iroquois officially would be neutral in the war, regarding it as a white man's conflict and waiting to see which side would prevail. Philip Schuyler, Oliver Wolcott, Turbutt Francis, and Volkert Douw comprised a commission sent to negotiate with the Confederacy. Schuyler presented the war to them as:

> A family quarrel between us and Old England. You Indians are not concerned in it. We don't wish you to take up the hatchet against the King's troops. We desire you to remain at home and not join on either side.[72]

The Iroquois chiefs agreed, but wanted in return munitions, blacksmiths, the expulsion of squatters, and for the Americans not to cross their territory to engage the British. All but the last of these terms were accepted. This situation would not long continue, however.

British officials, especially Sir William Johnson and, after his death, his son John and his nephew Guy, played on the past alliances with the Iroquois and the general Indian fear of the continual westward migration of the colonists. The Mohawk leader, Joseph Brant, a Christian educated in Lebanon, Connecticut, and commissioned in the British army, also was effective in drawing many Iroquois to the British side. The Oneida and at least half the Tuscaroras joined the Americans. Especially significant in the Oneida decision was the influence of Samuel Kirkland, a missionary and expert in their language and general culture. Also, the Oneidas, the Mohawks, and the Tuscaroras were oriented to Albany, the other tribes to British-controlled Fort Niagara. These economic and political considerations did carry weight. Of course, with the Mohawks, the influence of Brant was powerful.

The American victory and the treaties of 1784 and 1794 cost the Iroquois much of their land. Also war and disease had ravaged their numbers. No more would the Iroquois Confederacy be a major factor inhibiting expansion to the west.

After the American victory, New Yorkers, in particular, Philip Schuyler, former general and Jay's second cousin, began buying large amounts of land from the Indians and selling them for a tidy profit to white prospective settlers. A law passed by the U.S. Congress in 1793 stipulated that:

> No sale of lands made by any Indians, or any nation or tribe of Indians within the United States, shall be valid to any person or to any state ... unless

the same shall be made and duly executed at some public treaty held under the authority of the United States.[73]

The New Yorkers had no intention of being held back by this law. Two years later, the New York legislature enacted a law giving a majority of the five commissioners (Schuyler was one) the authority to

> Make such arrangements with the Oneida, Onondaga, and Cayuga tribes of Indians, respectively, relative to the lands appropriated to their use, as may tend to promote the interests of said Indians.[74]

This rather loose language certainly left the door open for shenanigans.

Secretary of War Timothy Pickering warned Governor Jay that any arrangements made by Schuyler would be invalid without approval by an agent of the United States government. Jay questioned the national law and further stated that the New York Constitution gave control of Indian affairs to the legislature, not to the governor. Although Jay was well aware that friends and allies

John Jay: The Forgotten Founder

of his were involved in the land deals, it is doubtful that this influenced his thinking. His record was one of not sacrificing principle to expediency and too he no longer was ambitious for higher office, increasingly, his thoughts were turning to retirement.

Jay did not hold views of white racial superiority, as was exemplified by his position on emancipation. His focus was on civilization, desiring to see both Indians and those of African origin move into Christian civilization and advance themselves educationally and economically. This thinking was shared by Joseph Brant who, although he stayed with the British after the war, rejecting the United States, was an Anglican who translated the New Testament and the Book of Common Prayer into Mohawk and wanted to see the Indians move into the modern world, adopting European ways. How different history would have been if people such as Jay and Brant controlled events.

The Character of John Jay

Retirement

My expectations from retirement have not been disappointed; and had Mrs. Jay continued with me, I should deem this the most agreeable part of my life.[75]

For many people, both in the time of John Jay and today, retirement means cessation from productive labor and spending the remaining years of life "smelling the roses." Today, a larger percentage of the population lives to the retirement years than in the early and mid-nineteenth century when Jay retired to his estate in Bedford, but the problem existed then as now, namely that too many people decide that they are entitled to a life of leisure. Although it is true that we humans need periods of rest and relaxation, God expects us to place service to Him at the top of our priorities as long as we are in this world.

Now that he was in his late fifties and slowing down physically, he was grateful for being out from under the pressures of public life. Even though he would be active in the ways discussed below, he did appreciate the slower pace of retirement. He wrote that:

The Character of John Jay

> Being retired from the fatigues and restraints of public life, I enjoy with real satisfaction the freedom and leisure which has at length fallen to my lot.[76]

He never forgot Sarah, always missed her, but was thankful for the blessings of what he had.

> Within a year after my removal to this place, I lost my faithful and affecttionate wife—I feel her absence. I have five children, and abundant reason to be thankful for them all.[77]

The property at Bedford had been acquired by Jay's maternal grandfather, Jacobus Van Cortland, back around 1700 and passed on to Jay by his father. Upon retiring from the governorship of New York, he added on to the house, creating a large, comfortable home with pleasant view from a slight rise across extensive lawns to low hills in the distance. He often expressed his deep love for the estate.

Once the adding on to the house project had been completed, Jay's life continued to be active concerning both estate business and spiritual, civic, and intellectual matters. In reference to the first category, he was interested in improving the output of the farm in order to generate more revenue and because of his wanting to learn better ways to do things. For example, he looked into finding improved fertilizers and ways to enhance the productivity of his farm land. As a result of his endeavors, he was elected a member of the Royal Agricultural Society of London, a rather fascinating indication of positive change in American/British relations since the end of the late war. Financially Jay was comfortable, but not so well off that income from the farm was of no significance. He had some inheritance from his father and had made some good real estate investments in New York City. His income from public service was good, albeit less than had he followed his father and grandfather into business. Still, all in all, his life in retirement was that of a country gentleman, if not a grandee.

Business concerns, though, did not keep Jay from actively showing his Christianity. He was a key leader in the establishing of St. Matthews Episcopal Church in Bedford where he served as warden. With his help, the parish erected a church building which still is there and engaged a priest.[78] In addition, he served as president of the American Bible Society, which had been founded in 1816 through the efforts of his son William, although by the time he accepted the office, 1821, his declining vigor precluded his doing much more than giving the organization the use of his name and writing an annual address.[79]

As Jay's health and energy gradually declined, his mind did not; he retained mental vigor and interest in many things. His faith was strong, especially his confidence in his salvation through Christ and the eternal life which lay ahead of him as a believer. He continued to care about and to be involved in a variety of civic and political matters. Many individuals, as they age, lose interest in the causes, events, and people in this world; they largely ignore these things and focus primarily on the next world. This Jay did not. He left an excellent example of how to age, how to handle the loss of physical vigor while continuing to be a useful servant of God. He rejoiced in the promise of heaven, but not to the exclusion of serving here and now.

Death

If in this life only we have hope in Christ, we are of all men the most pitiable.

But now Christ is risen from the dead, and has become the first fruits of those who have fallen asleep.[80]

    Jay died on May 17, 1829, at eighty-three years of age. He did his best to care for his health, but in the final analysis trusted fully in Christ's promise that His people would live eternally with Him. Certainly Christians are expected to use their rational faculties to do their best in all things, including providing for their health, but their ultimate trust is in God. Jay very much missed his wife who had died in 1802 and his physical vigor had declined during the 1820s. He did not, though, seek death. He enjoyed his family and his estate, understanding that length of days is in the hands of God. We humans do have control over how we face life and what we do when confronted by the vicissitudes of life. Jay's son, William, quoted the following advice his father passed on to the family:

> Cheerfulness promotes health, and health promotes cheerfulness. We are so formed, that when one part suffers, the rest, whether corporeal or mental, are in a degree affected by it. Hence it is the more proper, that we should attend to every indisposition, and to whatever may aggravate or prolong it.[81]

Jay integrated effectively spiritual health, mental health, and physical health. In addition to daily prayer and Bible reading with his family and visitors at Bedford, he loved being in the open air, frequently being out on horseback before breakfast.

Furthermore, as age and infirmity crept up on him, he did not become more inwardly turned as is the wont of some aging people, but rather, as William also observed, became more sensitive to others suffering difficulties and looked for ways to help them.[82]

In a letter written on January 23, 1827 to his old friend Peter Van Schaack, Jay realistically, almost matter of factly, discussed aging, but focused primarily on his faith.

> A kind Providence has extended our lives to the commencement of another year. Very few of our early associates remain with us. Our abode here is merely "pro hac vice," [for this occasion only] and our departure is then to place us in a state of eternal good or evil. That good can only be obtained by means of our merciful Redeemer, who was pleased to declare "without me, ye can do nothing."
>
> Although I have long been in a state of debility, yet it was lately so increased by an additional complaint, as caused me to delay preparing a few lines to you more seasonably.[83]

In his will too Jay set forth sound Christian principles expressing his appreciation to God for all the blessings of this world, yet cognizant that we depart it when He so wills and that it is our responsibility to be prepared for that call.

> I, John Jay, of Bedford, in the county of Westchester, and State of New York, being sensible of the importance and duty of so ordering my affairs as

to be prepared for death, do make and de-clare my last will and testament in manner and form following, viz:—Unto Him who is the author and giver of all good, I render sincere and humble thanks for his manifold and unmerited blessings, and especially for our redemption and salvation by his believed Son. He has been pleased to bless me with excellent parents, with a virtuous wife, and with worthy children. His protection has accompanied me through many eventful years, faithfully employed in the service of my country; and his providence has not only conducted me to this tranquil situation, but also given me abundant reason to be contented and thankful. Blessed be his holy name.[84]

It was not long before his death that he so wrote. This is a commendable testimony of Christian faith, combining enjoyment of this world with readiness to depart it when God summons us.

During his final days, he grew progressively weaker and could speak only with difficulty. He did manage to say to his widowed daughter Maria that "the Lord is good" and "the Lord is better than we deserve." In general, though, he was peacefully quiet, cared for by his daughters. Maria described the expression his face as "like a saint ripened for glory."[85] He was buried in the family cemetery at Rye, near the house where he had lived as a youth. On his tombstone was placed the following summary of a life well lived.

> In memory of John Jay, eminent among those who asserted the liberty and established the independence of his country, which he long served in the most important offices, legislative, executive, judicial and diplomatic, and distinguished in them all by his ability, firmness, patriotism, and integrity. He was in his life and death an example of the virtues, the faith and the hopes of a Christian.[86]

This was a wonderful tribute from his children for their father, an outstanding American patriot, one of the greatest of the founders, and a man who lived his Christianity to the end, leaving future generations many inspirations for both living well and dying well.

The Character of John Jay

End Notes

[1] James 2:26.

[2] Jay, *The Life of John Jay*, i, 398.

[3] *Ibid.*, i, 501.

[4] Norman Cousins, ed., *In God We Trust: The Religious Beliefs and Ideas of the American Founding Fathers* (New York: Harper and Brothers, 1958), 384.

[5] *Ibid.*, 362.

[6] Frank Monaghan, *John Jay: Defender of Liberty* (New York: The Bobbs-Merrill Company, 1935), 428.

[7] Frank Lambert, *The Founding Fathers and the Place of Religion in America* (Princeton, New Jersey: Princeton University Press, 2003), 181.

[8] *Ibid.*, 178.

[9] Jay, *The Life of John Jay*, i, 516.

[10] *Ibid.*, i, 516-517.

[11] Acts 26:20.

[12] Jay, *The Life of John Jay*, i, 518.

[13] Catherine Drinker Bowen, *John Adams and the American Revolution* (Boston: Little, Brown and Company, 1950), 479-480.

[14] Monaghan, *John Jay: Defender of Liberty*, 218.

[15] Jay, *The Life of John Jay*, 463.

[16] *Ibid.*, ii, 300.

[17] Edwin S. Gaustad, ed. *A Documentary History of Religion in America to the Civil War* (Grand Rapids, Michigan: William B. Eerdmans Publishing Company, 1993), 244.

End Notes: The Character of John Jay

[18] Manross, *A History of the American Episcopal Church*, 186.

[19] Stephen Neill, *Anglicanism* (Harmondsworth, Middlesex, England: Penguin Books, 1965), 227.

[20] Monaghan, *John Jay: Defender of Liberty*, 386-387.

[21] Russell Kirk, *Redeeming the Time* (Wilmington, Delaware: Intercollegiate Studies Institute, 1996), 67.

[22] Cousins, *In God We Trust*, 374.

[23] *Ibid.*, 370.

[24] *Ibid.*, 364.

[25] Edwin S. Gaustad, *Neither King Nor Prelate: Religion and the New Nation 1776-1826* (Grand Rapids, Michigan: William B. Eerdmans Publishing Company, 1993), 161.

[26] *Ibid.*, 164.

[27] *Ibid.*, 166.

[28] Joseph Story, *Commentaries on the Constitution of the United States*, 2nd ed., vol. II (Boston: Charles C. Little and James Brown, 1851), Sec. 1874, 593.

[29] Jay, *The Life of John Jay*, ii, 293.

[30] Gordon S. Wood, *The Radicalism of the American Revolution* (New York: Alfred A. Knopf, 1992), 299-300.

[31] Proverbs 13:1.

[32] Jay, *Correspondence and Public Papers*, i, 1.

[33] Russell Kirk, *America's British Culture* (New Brunswick, New Jersey: Transaction Publishers, 1993), 4.

[34] Stahr, *John Jay*, 13.

[35] Proverbs 31:10.

[36] Cokie Roberts, *Founding Mothers: The Women Who Raised Our Nation* (New York: Harper Collins Publishers, Inc., 2004), 440.

[37] Stahr, *John Jay*, 115.

[38] Proverbs 22:6.

[39] Stahr, *John Jay*, 282.

[40] Stephen P. Budney, *William Jay: Abolitionist and Anti-colonialist* (Westport, Connecticut: Praeger, 2005).

[41] Jay, *The Life of John Jay*, ii, 430.

[42] *Ibid.*, i, 23.

[43] *Ibid.*, ii, 124.

[44] *Ibid.*, ii, 131.

[45] Proverbs 18:24.

[46] Jay, *The Life of John Jay*, 175.

[47] *Ibid.*, 160.

[48] *Ibid.*, 161.

[49] *Ibid.*

[50] *Ibid.*, 355.

[51] Deuteronomy 31:6.

[52] Jay, *The Life of John Jay*, i, 398.

[53] *Ibid.*, ii, 385.

[54] *Ibid.*

[55] Stahr, *John Jay*, 25-27.

[56] Johnston, ed., *The Correspondence and Public Papers of John Jay*, i, 2.

[57] *Ibid.*, 11.

End Notes: The Character of John Jay

[58] Russell Kirk, *The Conservative Mind: From Burke to Eliot*, seventh revised edition (Washington, D.C.: Regnery Publishing, Inc., 2001), 8.

[59] Quoted in Peter Viereck, *Conservatism from John Adams to Churchill* (Princeton, New Jersey: D. Van Nostrand Company, Inc., 1956), 116-117.

[60] Jay, *The Life of John Jay*, ii, 330-331.

[61] Exodus 32:1-6.

[62] Percy, Lord Eustace, *The Heresy of Democracy: A Study in the History of Democracy* (Chicago: Henry Regnery Company, 1955), 26.

[63] Jay, *The Life of John Jay*, i, 71-72.

[64] *Ibid.*, ii, 398-399.

[65] *Ibid.*, i, 202-203.

[66] *Ibid.*, 279.

[67] *Ibid.*, ii, 285-286.

[68] *Ibid.*, i, 285.

[69] Stahr, *John Jay*, 193.

[70] Jay, *The Life of John Jay*, ii, 319.

[71] Colossians 3:11.

[72] William R. Nester, *The Frontier War for American Independence* (Mechanicsburg, Pennsylvania: Stackpole Books, 2004), 75.

[73] Stahr, *John Jay*, 348.

[74] *Ibid.*

[75] Jay, *The Life of John Jay*, i, 431.

[76] *Ibid.*, i, 431-432.

[77] *Ibid.*, i, 432.

[78] Stahr, *John Jay*, 378.
[79] *Ibid.*, 380.
[80] 1 Corinthians 15:19-20.
[81] Jay, *The Life of John Jay*, ii, 430.
[82] *Ibid.*, 462.
[83] *Ibid.*, 427.
[84] *Ibid.*, 519-520.
[85] Stahr, *John Jay*, 384.
[86] *Ibid.*, 387-388.

End Notes: The Character of John Jay

Part III: The Legacy of John Jay

A good name is to be chosen rather than great riches, loving favor rather than silver and gold.[1]

A proper history of the United States would have much to recommend it: in some respects it would be singular, or unlike all others; it would develop the great plan of Providence, for causing this extensive part of our world to be discovered, and these "uttermost parts of the earth" to be gradually filled with civilized and Christian people and nations.[2]

In evaluating the historical significance of Jay, Walter Stahr ranked him just after Franklin, Washington, Adams, Hamilton, Jefferson, and Madison—the order in which he listed them.[3] A better categorization would place Washington on a level by himself with the other six giants of the generation which won the war and established this country, arguably our greatest generation, standing together as the second tier. These men not only

The Legacy of John Jay

were effective revolutionaries, but also were successful builders of the new century.

Jay was a firm advocate of separation of powers and representative government with the franchise limited to the productive; he opposed both mass democracy on the one hand and rule by one person or a small group of people on the other. These elected representatives had the responsibility to administer government so as to protect order, justice, and freedom for all, not just for themselves. He did not believe that the mass of the people, if enfranchised, would preserve the civilized and free country he wanted to see grow and flourish.

In this, Jay was in line with the beliefs of Hamilton, Adams, and other key Federalist leaders. Among the opposition, there may have been philosophical disagreement with this view, but Jefferson and his followers did not in practice move that far from the Federalists. Substantial changes in the way the country was run were years in the future, at least until the presidency of Andrew Jackson who was elected to the first of two terms in 1828.

Of Jay, Samuel Flagg Bemis wrote words of praise that could be said of all too few public figures:

John Jay: The Forgotten Founder

> Of profound piety and unbreakable religious faith, unbending in patriotism, endeavoring always to keep an independent and evenly balanced political outlook, fond of good society, and with the strongest and most affectionate attachment for domestic life, Jay was a man on whose personal character the historical student may look back with pleasure.[4]

Allen Guelzo commented that Evangelical Episcopalians in the United States did not produce lay leaders corresponding to those in the Church of England such as Wilberforce, Shaftesbury, and the Clapham sect. In the United States, John Jay and Francis Scott Key were the most impressive of a slimmer number.[5]

In praising Jay, Richard B. Morris raises problems for many readers today. He stated:

> While his service to the nation in foreign affairs was of longer duration and has perhaps left a stamp more durable, he utilized the High Court to provide an audaciously nationalistic exposition of the Constitution, one that has been reaffirmed and applied

in areas beyond the purview of the Founding Fathers. By character, training, and experience he was peculiarly fitted to occupy the posts of responsibility and decision-making that he filled during a period when the national government cried out for energetic and bold direction and an outlook that was continental rather than provincial.

Rather than as a technician of the law, Jay is remembered as a creative statesman and activist Chief Justice whose concepts of the broad purpose and powers of the Constitution were to be upheld and spelled out with boldness and vigor by John Marshall.[6]

Certainly there is truth in commending Jay for his character, abilities, and contribution to the establishment and early life of this country. He was a strong chief justice who believed in the necessity for a strong central government. The description of him as an "activist Chief Justice," however, today raises the specter of one who ignores Constitutional statements in pursuit of a personal agenda. Jay determined to keep the

Supreme Court out of political matters, focusing on its judicial responsibilities. Too often today and in recent years courts instead decide to impose their views, seeking, in effect, to legislate what the law of the land should be. This imbalance in the relationship between the executive, legislative, and judicial branches is not, however, unprecedented. During each period of U.S. history, one of the branches has asserted itself too strongly, threatening the balance. Those who value order, justice and freedom must be alert constantly and redress the balance whenever necessary.

While it is manifestly impossible to study Jay's public life and positively infer what he would have done in future circumstances, it is difficult to believe that he would have found in the Constitution any basis for ruling with the majority in cases such as Roe v. Wade which established the legal right of women to kill their unborn children. Nor can one envision him with the majority in Engel v. Vitale which struck down state sponsored prayer in public schools, Abington School District v. Schempp which prohibited devotional Bible reading in these schools, or in Stone v. Graham which forbade the posting of the Ten Commandments in public school classrooms.

Although Jay was a broad constructionist who did want to expand the powers of the United

States government, it is unlikely that his rulings would ever go to the extremes discussed above. His Christian worldview and his high regard for the Constitution no doubt would have precluded his supporting these and other examples of secularist judicial usurpation.

After his death, Jay's sons found among his papers an extensive prayer which included the following words summarizing his convictions. His Christianity was not just personal but also acknowledged that nations too are subject to God and responsible to be obedient to Him.

> Be pleased to bless me and my family, my friends and enemies, and all for whom I ought to pray, in the manner and measure which thou and thou only, knowest to be best for us. Create in us all clean and contrite, and thankful hearts, and renew within us a right spirit.
>
> I thank thee, the great Sovereign of the universe, for thy long-continued goodness to these countries, notwithstanding our ingratitude and disobedience to thee, our merciful deliverer and benefactor. Give us grace to turn

unto thee with true repentance, and implore thy forgiveness. And be pleased to forgive us; and bless us with such portions of prosperity as thou seest to be fit for us, and with rulers who fear thee, and walk in the paths which our Saviour hath set before us. Be pleased to bless all nations with the knowledge of thy gospel,—and may thy holy will be done on earth as it is in heaven.

Give me grace to meditate with faith and gratitude on thy kind redeeming love all the days of my life. When thou shalt call me hence, be with me in the hour of death, and bless me with a full assurance of faith and hope, that I may "fear no evil."[7]

To the best of his ability, he lived these words. May God continue to bless us with leaders such as John Jay, people of sound intellect and courage grounded in Christianity.

The Legacy of John Jay

The Lessons of Leadership

Leaders follow God.
God brings opportunities; leaders know what to do with them.
Leaders cannot lead unless someone follows.
Leaders, though, do not worry about numbers.
Principle comes before popularity.
Leaders are motivated by ideals.
They operate, however, in the context of reality.
Leaders know how to win in stages, when to settle for a partial victory now.
Leaders never give up.
They are strengthened by adversity.
They learn from failure.
Private character and public character should coincide.
Leaders analyze carefully, then act decisively.
Leaders know when to wait and when to act.
Leaders know their limitations.
They never stop learning.
Leaders will listen to others.
Leaders protect their health.
Leaders can inspire others to excel.
Leaders are more interested in success than in fame.

The Legacy of John Jay

But, they are not spoiled by their success.
How one leads in his family indicates how he will lead the country.
Leaders master detail, but know when to delegate.
Leaders are optimistic.
They are excited by challenges.
Good ends cannot be gained through bad means.
Leaders can bring people together without sacrificing principle.
Leaders control their emotions rather than being controlled by them.
Those who lead today must understand yesterday and anticipate eagerly tomorrow.
A leader takes seriously his cause, not himself.

End Notes

[1] Proverbs 22:1.

[2] Jay, *The Life of John Jay*, ii, 320-321.

[3] Stahr, *John Jay*, 387.

[4] Bemis, *Jay's Treaty*, 281.

[5] Allen C. Guelzo, *For the Union of Evangelical Christendom: The Irony of the Reformed Episcopalians* (University Park, Pennsylvania: The Pennsylvania State University Press, 1994), 42.

[6] Morris, *Witnesses at the Creation*, 259-260.

[7] Jay, *The Life of John Jay*, ii, 518-519.

End Notes: The Legacy of John Jay

BIBLIOGRAPHY

Primary Sources

Burke, Edmund. *Selected Writings and Speeches*, ed. by Peter J. Stanlis. Chicago: Regnery Gateway, 1963.

Commager, Henry Steele and Morris, Richard B., eds. *The Spirit of 'Seventy-six: The Story of the American Revolution as Told by Participants.* New York: Bonanza Books, 1958.

Cousins, Norman, ed. *In God We Trust: The Religious Beliefs and Ideas of the American Founding Fathers.* New York: Harper and Brothers, 1958.

Crary, Catherine S. ed. *The Price of Loyalty: Tory Writings from the Revolutionary Era.* New York: McGraw-Hill Book Company, 1973.

Bibliography

Gaustad, Edwin S., ed. *A Documentary History of Religion in America to the Civil War*. Grand Rapids, Michigan: William B. Eerdmans Publishing Company, 1993.

Hamilton, Alexander; Madison, James, and Jay, John. *The Federalist Papers*. New York: Mentor, 1961.

Jay, John. *The Correspondence and Public Papers of John Jay*, ed. by Henry P. Johnston. 4 vols. New York: Burt Franklin, 1880-1883.

Jay, William. *The Life of John Jay: With Selections From His Correspondence and Miscellaneous Papers*. Bridgewater, Virginia: American Foundation Publications, 2000.

Morris, Richard, ed. John Jay: *The Making of a Revolutionary* [Unpublished Papers 1745-1780]. New York: Harper and Row Publishers, 1975.

Rhodehamel, John, ed. *George Washington: Writings*. New York: The Library of America, 1997.

Rousseau, Jean Jacques. *The Social Contract*. Vol. 38 of *Great Books of the Western World*, editor-in-chief Robert Maynard Hutchins. Chicago: Encyclopedia Britannica, Inc., 1952.

Bibliography

Secondary Sources

Ackerman, Bruce. *The Failure of the Founding Fathers: Jefferson, Marshall, and the Rise of Presidential Democracy*. Cambridge, Massachusetts: The Belknap Press of Harvard University Press, 2005.

Adams, William Howard. *Gouverneur Morris: An Independent Life*. New Haven, Connecticut: Yale University Press, 2003.

Alsop, Susan Mary. *Yankees at the Court: The First Americans in Paris*. Garden City, New York: Doubleday and Company, Inc., 1982.

Bellamy, Francis. *The Private Life of George Washington*. New York: Thomas Y. Crowell Company, 1951.

Belmonte, Kevin. *Hero For Humanity: A Biography of William Wilberforce*. Colorado Springs, Colorado: NavPress, 2002.

Bibliography

Bemis, Samuel Flagg. *Jay's Treaty: A Study in Commerce and Diplomacy.* New Haven, Connecticut: Yale University Press, 1962.

Bowen, Catherine Drinker. *John Adams and the American Revolution.* Boston: Little, Brown and Company, 1950.

_____. *Miracle at Philadelphia: The Story of the Constitutional Convention May to September 1787.* Boston: Little, Brown and Company, 1966.

Brodsky, Alyn. *Benjamin Rush: Patriot and Physician.* New York: St. Martin's Press, 2004.

Brookhiser, Richard. *Alexander Hamilton: American.* New York: The Free Press, 1999.

Brown, Harold O. J. *The Reconstruction of the Republic.* New Rochelle, New York: Arlington House, 1977.

Budney, Stephen P. *William Jay: Abolitionist and Anti-colonialist*. Westport: Connecticut: Praeger, 2005.

Butler, Jon. *Becoming American: The Revolution before 1776*. Cambridge, Massachusetts: Harvard University Press, 2000.

Callahan, North. *Flight from the Republic: The Forms of the American Revolution*. Indianapolis, Indiana: The Bobbs-Merrill Company, Inc., 1967.

Carson, Clarence B. *The Rebirth of Liberty: The Founding of the American Republic 1760-1800*. New Rochelle, New York: Arlington House, 1973.

Chadwick, Bruce. *George Washington's War: The Forging of a Revolutionary Leader and the American Presidency*. Naperville, Illinois: Sourcebooks, Inc., 2004.

Chernow, Ron. *Alexander Hamilton*. New York: The Penguin Press, 2004.

Churchill, Winston S. *A History of the English Speaking Peoples*. Vol. III: *The Age of Revo-*

lution. London: Cassell and Company Ltd., 1957.

Cook, Dan. *The Long Fuse: How England Lost the American Colonies 1760-1785*. New York: The Atlantic Monthly Press, 1995.

De Gregorio, William A. *The Complete Book of U.S. Presidents: From George Washington to George W. Bush*. New York: Barnes and Noble Books, 2004.

Diamant, Lincoln. *Chaining the Hudson: The Fight for the River in the American Revolution*. New York: Carol Publishing Group, 1989.

Dull, Jonathan R. *A Diplomatic History of the American Revolution*. New Haven, Connecticut: Yale University Press, 1985.

Eidsmoe, John. *Christianity and the Constitution: The Faith of our Founding Fathers*. Grand Rapids, Michigan: Baker Books, 1987.

Elkins, Stanley and Mr. Kitrick, Eric. *The Age of Federalism*. New York: Oxford University Press, 1993.

Ellis, Joseph S. *Founding Brothers: The Revolutionary Generation.* New York: Vintage Books, 2000.

———. *Passionate Sage: The Character and Legacy of John Adams.* New York: W. W. Norton and Company, 1993.

Ferling, John. *Adams vs. Jefferson: The Tumultuous Election of 1800.* New York: Oxford University Press, 2004.

———. *A Leap in the Dark: The Struggle to Create the American Republic.* New York: Oxford University Press, 2003.

Fleming, Thomas. *Duel: Alexander Hamilton, Aaron Burr and the Future of America.* New York: Basic Books, 1999.

———. *Washington's Secret War: The Hidden History of Valley Forge.* New York: Smithsonian Books, 2005.

Flexner, James Thomas. *George Washington in the American Revolution (1775-1783).* Boston: Little, Brown and Company, 1968.

_____. *The Young Hamilton.* Boston: Little Brown and Company, 1978.

Freeman, Douglas Southall. *George Washington.* 7 vols.; New York: Charles Scribner's Sons, 1951.

Fuller, J. F. C. *Decisive Battles of the U.S.A.* New York: Thomas Youseloff, Inc., 1942.

_____. *A Military History of the Western World,* Vol. II: *From the Defeat of the Spanish Armada, 1588, to the Battle of Waterloo, 1815.* New York: Funk and Wagnalls Company, 1955.

Guelzo, Allen C. *For the Union of Evangelical Christendom: The Story of the Reformed Episcopalians.* University Park, Pennsylvania: The Pennsylvania State University Press, 1994.

Harper, John Lamberton. *American Machiavelli: Alexander Hamilton and the Origins of American Foreign Policy.* Cambridge, United Kingdom: Cambridge University Press, 2004.

Hefley, James C. *America: One Nation Under God.* Wheaton, Illinois: Victor Books. 1975.

Hutchinson, William R. *Religious Pluralism in America: The Contentious History of a Founding Ideal.* New Haven, Connecticut: Yale University Press, 2003.

Isaacson, Walter. *Benjamin Franklin: An American Life.* New York: Simon and Schuster, 2003.

Johnson, Herbert Alan. *John Jay 1745-1829.* Albany, New York: New York State American Bicentennial Commission, 1976.

Johnson, Paul. *A History of the American People.* New York: Harper Collins Publishers, 1997.

Kagan, Robert. *Dangerous Nation.* New York: Alfred A. Knopf, 2006.

Kirk, Russell. *America's British Culture.* New Brunswick, New Jersey: Transaction Publishers, 1993.

———. *The Conservative Constitution.* Washington, D.C.: Regnery Gateway, 1990.

_____. *The Conservative Mind: From Burke to Eliot.* Seventh revised edition. Washington, D.C.: Regnery Publishing, Inc., 2001.

_____. *Redeeming the Time.* Wilmington, Delaware: Intercollegiate Studies Institute, 1996.

Lambert, Frank. *The Founding Fathers and the Place of Religion in America.* Princeton, New Jersey: Princeton University Press, 2003.

McCullough, David. *John Adams.* New York: Simon and Schuster, 2001.

McDonald, Forrest. *E Pluribus Unum.* Indianapolis, Indiana: Liberty Press, 1965.

Maine, Sir Henry Sumner. *Popular Government.* Indianapolis, Indiana: Liberty Classics, 1976.

Manross, William Wilson. *A History of the American Episcopal Church.* New York: Morehouse Publishing Co., 1935.

Marshall, Peter and Manuel, David. *The Light and the Glory.* Old Tappan, New Jersey: Fleming H. Revell Company, 1977.

Middlekauff, Robert. *The Glorious Cause: The American Revolution 1763-1789*. New York: Oxford University Press, 2005.

Miller, John C. *Alexander Hamilton and the Growth of the New Nation*. New York: Harper Torchbooks, 1964.

Monaghan, Frank. *John Jay: Defender of Liberty*. New York: The Bobbs-Merrill Company, 1935.

Morgan, Edmund. *Benjamin Franklin*. New Haven, Connecticut: Yale University Press, 2003.

Morison, Samuel Eliot. *The Oxford History of the American People*. New York: Oxford University Press, 1965.

Morris, Richard B. *The Forging of the Union 1781-1789*. New York: Harper and Row, Publishers, 1987.

_____. John Jay: *The Winning of the Peace 1780-1784*. New York: Harper and Row, Publishers, 1980.

_____. *The Peacemakers: The Great Powers and American Independence.* New York: Harper and Row, Publishers, 1965.

_____. *Witness at the Creation: Hamilton, Madison, Jay and the Constitution.* New York: Holt, Rinehart and Winston, 1985.

Neill, Stephen. *Anglicanism.* Harmondsworth, Middlesex, England: Penguin Books, 1965.

Nelson, Craig. *Thomas Paine: Enlightenment, Revolution, and the Birth of Modern Nations.* New York: Viking, 2006.

Nester, William R. *The Frontier War for American Independence.* Mechanicsburg, Pennsylvania: Stackpole Books, 2004.

Noll, Mark A. *A History of Christianity in the United States and Canada.* Grand Rapids, Michigan: William B. Eerdmans Company, 1992.

North, Gary. *Political Polytheism: The Myth of Pluralism.* Tyler, Texas: Institute for Christian Economics, 1989.

Percy, Lord. *The Heresy of Democracy: A Study in the History of Democracy*. Chicago: Henry Regnery Company, 1955.

Phillips, Kevin. *The Cousins' Wars: Religion, Politics and the Triumph of Anglo-America*. New York: Basic Books, 1999.

Rakove, John N. *Original Meanings: Politics and Ideas in the Making of the Constitution*. New York: Alfred A Knopf, 1997.

Randall, Willard Sterne. *George Washington: A Life*. New York: Henry Holt and Company, 1997.

Roberts, Cokie. *Founding Mothers: The Women Who Raised Our Nation*. New York: Harper Collins Publishers, Inc., 2004.

Robertson, Pat. *America's Dates with Destiny*. Nashville, Tennessee: Thomas Nelson Publishers, 1986.

Roosevelt, Theodore. *The Works of Theodore Roosevelt*. Vol. IX: *The Winning of the West*. New York: Charles Scribner's Sons, 1926.

Bibliography

Rushdoony, Rousas J. *This Independent Republic: Studies in the Nature of American History.* Nutley, New Jersey: The Craig Press, 1964.

Siemers, David J. *The Antifederalists: Men of Great Faith and Forbearance.* Lanham, Maryland: Rowman and Littlefield Publishers, Inc., 2003.

Smith, Gary Scott, ed. *God and Politics: Four Views on the Reformation of Civil Government.* Phillipsburg, New Jersey: Presbyterian and Reformed Publishing Company, 1989.

Smith, Richard Norton. *Patriarch: George Washington and the New American Nation.* Boston: Houghton Mifflin Company, 1993.

Stahr, Walter. *John Jay: Founding Father.* New York: Hambledon and London, 2005.

Stiles, Francis N. *John Marshall: Defender of the Constitution.* Boston: Little, Brown and Company, 1981.

Story, Joseph. *Commentaries on the Constitution of the United States*, 2nd ed., vol. II. Boston: Charles C. Little and James Brown, 1851.

Unger, Harlow Giles. *Lafayette*. Hoboken, New Jersey: John Wiley and Sons, Inc., 2002.

Viereck, Peter: *Conservatism: From John Adams to Churchill*. Princeton: New Jersey: D. Van Nostrand Company, Inc., 1956.

Weinberger, Jerry. *Benjamin Franklin Unmasked: On the Unity of His Moral, Religious, and Political Thought*. Lawrence, Kansas: University Press of Kansas, 2005.

Wood, Gordon S. *The Radicalism of the American Revolution*. New York: Alfred A. Knopf, 1992.

Bibliography

About the Author

John M. Pafford is an ordained clergyman and has been a professor of history at Northwood University in Midland, Michigan since 1976. In 1995, Dr. Pafford received the Northwood University Award for Faculty Excellence.

Among other positions, Dr. Pafford has served as chairman of the Michigan Republican Issues Committee, co-chairman of Michigan Scholars for Reagan-Bush, and is a member of the Board of Scholars of the Mackinac Center for Public Policy. Back in the 1960s, he was chairman of Young Americans for Freedom in two states.

He is the author of five books, numerous articles on history, theology, and contemporary events and is an experienced speaker.

www.ingramcontent.com/pod-product-compliance
Lightning Source LLC
Chambersburg PA
CBHW060552230426
43670CB00011B/1796